THE **MINI** ROUGH GUIDE TO
IRELAND

YOUR TAILOR-MADE TRIP
STARTS HERE

Tailor-made trips and unique adventures crafted by local experts

Rough Guides has been inspiring travellers for more than 35 years. Leave it to our local experts to create your perfect itinerary and book it at local rates.

Don't follow the crowd – find your own path.

HOW ROUGHGUIDES.COM/TRIPS WORKS

STEP 1 Pick your dream destination, tell us what you want and submit an enquiry.

STEP 2 Fill in a short form to tell your local expert about your dream trip and preferences.

STEP 3 Our local expert will craft your tailor-made itinerary. You'll be able to tweak and refine it until you're completely satisfied.

STEP 4 Book online with ease, pack your bags and enjoy the trip. Our local expert will be on hand 24/7 while you're on the road.

PLAN AND BOOK YOUR TRIP AT
ROUGHGUIDES.COM/TRIPS

HOW TO DOWNLOAD YOUR FREE EBOOK

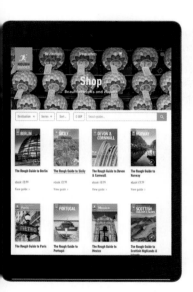

1. Visit **www.roughguides.com/free-ebook** or scan the **QR code** below

2. Enter the code **ireland731**

3. Follow the simple step-by-step instructions

For troubleshooting contact: mail@roughguides.com

10 THINGS NOT TO MISS

A PERFECT TOUR

Day 1

Dublin. Walk the streets of Georgian Dublin, from Trinity College's cobbled quadrangle to the wide expanse of Merrion Square, then enjoy a light lunch at the National Gallery. Cross the Ha'penny Bridge and follow O'Connell Street to Parnell Square and the Dublin Writers Museum.

Day 2

Kilkenny and Tipperary. Leave Dublin by car for Kilkenny — founded by St Canice in the sixth century — and Kilkenny Castle, a magnificent edifice in rich parkland beside the River Nore. Have lunch at the Kilkenny Design Centre, an emporium of Irish crafts. Drive on to Tipperary and climb the Rock of Cashel, to savour its magnificent ruins.

Day 3

Cork City. Explore Cork's city centre on foot, lunching in the vast covered food market. Then take a twenty-minute train ride to the port of Cobh, the last sight of home for generations of emigrants, whose tale is told at The Queenstown Story in Cobh Heritage Centre.

Day 4

Coast path to Killarney. The west Cork coastal road (N71) meanders through tiny villages, where the pubs showcase local artisan foods, to the treasure-packed Bantry House, and sub-tropical Glengarriff. Drive through Kenmare to Moll's Gap for a jaw-dropping scenic approach to Killarney.

Day 5 & 6

Kerry. Explore the lakes and heather-clad mountains

of Killarney. The Gap of Dunloe excursion includes a lake cruise, join it at Ross Castle.

Day 7

Cliffs of Moher. At Lahinch, you can surf the same Atlantic breakers that pound the nearby Cliffs of Moher. Warm up with Irish stew in Doolin while foot-tapping to live Irish music, and consider a day trip to the Aran Islands, or a visit to the Burren's numerous megalithic remains.

Day 8

The wild west. Drive west from Galway to Connemara, a sparsely populated wilderness of bog, scattered blue lakes, and distant purple mountains. Enjoy the seafood in Clifden, then head for Connemara National Park. Hike up Diamond Hill for a panoramic view.

Day 9

The Antrim Coast. Marvel at the Giant's Causeway's bizarre basalt columns, as have generations of visitors. Enjoy the cosy inn at Bushmills (see page 106), next door to Ireland's oldest distillery. Nearby are the evocative clifftop ruins of Dunluce Castle.

Day 10

Belfast. An impressive Victorian city with chic bars and restaurants, and quirky museums and libraries, Belfast is a popular weekend break destination, with friendly locals, known for their down-to-earth sense of humour. Visit Titanic Belfast, birthplace of the ill-fated liner, to explore the history of the Titanic, and understand the local pride in the city's industrial past.

CONTENTS

A NOTE TO READERS

At Rough Guides, we always strive to bring you the most up-to-date information. This book was produced during a period of continuing uncertainty caused by the Covid-19 pandemic, so please note that content is more subject to change than usual. We recommend checking the latest restrictions and official guidance.

OVERVIEW

The grass really does grow greener in Ireland – it's not called the 'Emerald Isle' for nothing. Ireland is a small country, and one to savour slowly. The quick-changing sky adds to the drama of the encounter between land and sea. You're never further than 115km (70 miles) from Ireland's dramatic 4,800-km (3,000-mile) coastline. Far to the west lies America, a beacon for countless emigrants during the nineteenth century. To the east lies Britain, whose relationship with its next door neighbour has for 800 years been one of the most sensitive and dramatic in European geo-politics; the negotiations surrounding Brexit and the so-called 'Irish backstop' providing the latest chapter in this ongoing saga.

The proximity of the Gulf Stream keeps winters in Ireland mild. Snow is rare, rain is not. Significant rainfall is recorded on three out of every four days near the west coast, and on every second day in the east, ranging from stormy torrents to refreshing mists so nebulous that they leave the streets unmarked. Sunshine is rarely far behind, however.

There are, of course, two Irelands – the 26 counties of the Republic and the

Emigration

Almost 7 million people live on the island – fewer than before the Great Famine of the 1840s. Emigration was high until the 'Celtic Tiger' boom, when jobs in new industries kept locals at home. The economy nosedived in 2008, but had recovered its feet by 2016, only for Brexit to unleash another wave of uncertainty. Applications for Irish passports by second-generation Irish living in Britain soared as the UK prepared to leave the EU.

six counties of Northern Ireland (each with their own government) – and two capitals: Dublin and Belfast. Dublin is a lively city of broad avenues, green parks, and cultural attractions, buzzing with creative energy and a delightfully subversive sense of humour. Belfast, historically Ireland's industrial centre, is a little more grounded, but undergoing its own renaissance.

Crohy Head Sea Arch

Largely, though, the truly inspiring sights are found outside the big towns. Natural wonders in Ireland can be as awesome as the Cliffs of Moher, or as tranquil as the Lakes of Killarney; as mystical as the holy mountain of Croagh Patrick, or as delightful as the horse-breeding pastures of the Curragh. Scattered amid these natural beauties stand impressive stone relics dating back thousands of years. It was here that remote monastic settlements kept learning alive in Europe during the Dark Ages.

Formerly one of Europe's most conservative corners, with the Catholic Church holding sway in the Republic and fundamentalist Presbyterians powerful in the North, Irish society as a whole has been transformed by progressive politics in the last decade, with divorce, gay marriage and abortion now legal (as of October 2019 in the case of Northern Ireland) on both sides of the border. Once an island synonymous with emigration, Ireland now welcomes immigrants from around the world.

Gorgeous coastline along Slea Head Drive

THE IRISH

More than 1.4 million people live in Dublin, the largest city in the Republic, and home to over a quarter of its population. Belfast, with a metropolitan population of around 635,000, is the hub of Northern Ireland, which remained part of the United Kingdom when the island was partitioned after the Irish War of Independence. Southern Ireland (Éire, latterly the Republic of Ireland), whose birth pangs in 1922 included a civil war, settled down to being a predominantly rural economy, with social affairs and its education system strongly influenced by the Catholic Church.

In the final quarter of the twentieth century, as Northern Ireland was suffering political turmoil, the South transformed itself into a modern European state. A strong youth culture turned Dublin into a party town targeted for weekend breaks by Europe's budget airlines. The 1998 Good Friday Agreement ushered in a period of peace and prosperity in the North, although the collapse of the power-sharing agreement between Republicans and Unionists meant the devolved government stopped functioning in 2017. Concerns that the stability of the region will be threatened by Brexit have dominated politics on both sides of the border since 2016.

A NATIVE TONGUE

Centuries of imposed rule from Britain led to the imposition of the English language over Gaelic, which was outlawed. According to the 2016 census, 1.7 million people speak the Irish language, with varying degrees of fluency. Reviving Gaelic – or Irish, as it is usually called – has become state policy; it is taught in schools and printed (along with English) on all official signs and documents. Indeed, in some Gaelic-speaking (Gaeltacht) areas, road signs are in Gaelic only, which can make life difficult for tourists. Irish-medium schools are increasingly popular in both urban and rural Ireland, bringing the Irish language outside of its traditional heartland. Its vocabulary, intonation, and sentence structures have infiltrated the English spoken here, creating great literature and lending everyday speech a touch of poetry.

THE NORTHERN COUNTIES

For the last three decades of the twentieth century, the image of Northern Ireland was tarnished by the violent sectarian conflict, known as 'The Troubles', between Protestant Unionists and Catholic Republicans. Since the Good Friday Agreement was signed in 1998, a more harmonious co-existence prevails, although animosities can still be ignited, particularly around 'marching season' (April–August). Brexit has also caused uncertainty about future peace prospects, with fears that a hard border may return. In spite of its turbulent past, residents here are down-to-earth, humorous and friendly, and the scenery is spectacular.

HISTORY AND CULTURE

Stone-Age relics reveal that Ireland has been inhabited since 8,000 BC. The first settlers probably travelled on foot from Scandinavia to Scotland – Britain was once linked to northern Europe by land – then across the narrow sea gap to Ireland.

Stone Age tombs and temples are strewn across the country, from simple stone tripods in farmer's fields to sophisticated passage-graves built on astronomical principles and decorated with mysterious engravings. New settlers introduced Bronze-Age skills from Europe, but the Iron Age arrived in Ireland relatively late.

The Roman legions that rolled across Western Europe into Britain stopped at the Irish Sea and Ireland was left to develop its own way of life during the centuries of the great Roman Empire. Though Irish society comprised scores of oft-feuding mini-kingdoms, a single culture did develop. Druids and poets told legends in a common tongue clearly identifiable as an early form of the Irish language, which later gave rise to Scots Gaelic and Manx.

A saint's success

St Patrick's crusade was a unique triumph. Ireland was the only Western European country where the local people were converted without a single Christian being martyred.

ST PATRICK'S DAY

The Celts frequently staged raids on Roman Britain for booty and slaves. During one fifth-century sortie, they took a 16-year-old boy named Patrick captive. After spending a few years as a humble shepherd, he escaped to Gaul, became a monk, returned to convert 'the heathens' to Christianity and ultimately became one of Ireland's three patron saint. On this remote, rural and scantly populated island, St Patrick and his successors developed a system of monasteries which kept the flame of Western culture alight while the rest of Europe fumbled through the Dark Ages. Scholarly minds from around Europe converged on the 'island of saints and scholars' to participate in its

Bronze cast of Vikings Strongbow and Aoife, Waterford

religious and intellectual life; Irish monks created beautiful illuminated manuscripts, while others travelled to Britain and mainland Europe, founding monasteries.

THE VIKINGS

At the turn of the ninth century, heavily-armed warriors sailed in from Scandinavia aboard sleek boats. The defenceless Irish monasteries, full of relics and treasures, were easy targets. The Vikings' shallow-draught ships moved in quickly and attacked at will, making their way around the Irish coast and up the country's rivers. This danger inspired the building of multi-storey 'round towers', which variously served as watchtowers, belfries, storehouses, and places of refuge (the remains of 65 such towers still stand). The Vikings also established trading colonies around the coast and founded Ireland's first major settlements: Dublin, Waterford and Limerick.

While the Irish learned sailing, weaponry, and metalworking from the Norse, they resented their presence. In the end, the natives ousted the Vikings, with the last clash taking place in 1014 at the Battle of Clontarf, when the High King of Ireland, BrianBorú, defeated the Norse and their Irish allies, although he himself was killed in the battle.

RIVALRY AND REVENGE

Ireland's next invasion was motivated by jealousy. In 1152, the wife of Tiernan O'Rourke, an Irish warrior king, was carried off by rival Dermot MacMurrough of Leinster. Allegedly the lady was a willing victim, possibly even the instigator. O'Rourke got his queen back a few months later and forced Dermot to flee, first to England in 1166, and then France. But from there, Dermot was able to shape an alliance with a powerful Norman nobleman, the Earl of Pembroke. The Earl, known as Strongbow, agreed to lead an army to sweep Dermot back to power. In exchange, the Earl was to be given the hand of Dermot's daughter and the right to succeed him to the Leinster throne. The hardy Normans – the elite of Europe's warrior cultures – won the Battle of Waterford in 1170, and Strongbow married his princess in Waterford's grand cathedral. In further engagements, the Norman war machine stunned, and swiftly defeated Viking and Irish forces. Things were going so well for Strongbow that his overlord, King Henry II of England, arrived in 1171 to assert his sovereignty.

THE ENGLISH ASCENDANCY

The Anglo-Norman occupation brought profound and long-lasting changes. Towns, churches and castles were built alongside institutions for feudal government. There was much resentment among the Irish, but for the colonial rulers the challenge of revolt was less serious than the danger of total cultural assimilation.

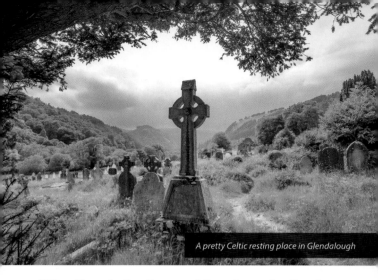

A pretty Celtic resting place in Glendalough

With settlers adopting the ways of the natives, rather than the other way round, the Statutes of Kilkenny were introduced in 1366, banning intermarriage and forbidding the English from speaking Gaelic.

English control was consolidated when the House of Tudor turned its attention to Ireland. Henry VIII, the first English monarch to be titled 'King of Ireland', introduced the Reformation to Ireland, but Protestantism took root only in the Pale (the area around Dublin) and in the large provincial towns under English control. In the rest of Ireland, Catholic monasteries carried on as before, as did the Irish language.

From the mid–sixteenth century, the implementation of the so-called plantation policy heralded the large-scale redistribution of wealth. Desirable farmland was confiscated from Catholics and given to Protestant settlers. During the reign of Elizabeth I, revolts were widespread, but the most unyielding resistance

Emigration statue, County Cork

was in the northeastern province of Ulster – Irish chieftains formed an alliance with the Queen's bitter enemy, Spain, and in 1601, a Spanish mini-armada sailed into the southern port of Kinsale. The English defeated the invaders, and many of the Irish earls were exiled to Europe. During the reign of James I, most of the north was confiscated and 'planted' with thousands of Scots and English, who changed the face of the province. After the English Civil War, Oliver Cromwell ruthlessly massacred the garrisons at Drogheda and Wexford in retribution for their support of Charles I, and pursued his own colonisation of Ireland. From 1654, Catholics were only allowed to hold land west of the River Shannon, much of it scarcely habitable. 'To Hell or to Connaught' was the slogan used to sum up the dilemma for the dispossessed.

After the religious war that culminated in the Battle of the Boyne, the Irish Catholic majority was subjected to further persecution in the form of the Penal Laws, introduced by the all-Protestant Irish parliament and designed to keep Catholics away from positions of power and influence.

REVOLUTIONARY IDEAS

It took the American Revolution to inspire daring new thinking in Ireland, with Henry Grattan leading agitation for greater freedom and tolerance. A Protestant of aristocratic heritage, Grattan staunchly defended the rights of all Irishmen in the House of Commons. Further pressure came from an Irish Protestant, Theobald Wolfe Tone, a young lawyer campaigning for parliamentary reform and the abolition of anti-Catholic laws. In 1793 Catholic landholders won the vote and other concessions thanks to Tone. In 1798 a French squadron came to the aid of Tone's United Irishmen off the coast of Cork. It was swiftly intercepted by British naval forces and Wolfe Tone was captured. Convicted of treason, he slit his throat before his sentence of death by hanging could be carried out.

In 1801 the Irish Parliament voted itself out of business by approving the Act of Union, which established the United Kingdom of Great Britain and Ireland. All Irish MPs would now sit at Westminster. In 1823, Daniel O'Connell founded the Catholic Association to work for emancipation. Five years later, he won a seat in the House of Commons, but as a Catholic was legally forbidden to take it. To prevent conflict, Parliament passed the Roman Catholic Relief Act (1829), removing the most discriminatory laws and paving the way for Catholic Emancipation.

BATTLE OF THE BOYNE

Ireland became the battleground for an English power struggle when William of Orange, a Dutch Protestant, challenged his father-in-law (and uncle), the Catholic James II, for the British throne. From exile in France, James sailed to Ireland to mobilise allies and met William's army in July 1690 at the River Boyne. The Orangemen, aided by troops from several Protestant countries, vastly outnumbered the Irish and French forces. The anniversary of William's victory is still celebrated with fervour by Protestants in Northern Ireland.

Leo Varadkar

STARVATION AND EMIGRATION

One of the worst disasters of nineteenth-century Europe was the Great Famine. In September 1845, potato blight was found on farms in southeast Ireland. The British government set up an investigation, but the outbreak was misdiagnosed. The next crop failed across Ireland, wiping out the staple food of the Irish peasant. Cruel winter weather and the outbreak of disease added to the horror of starvation. Believing that they should not interfere with free market forces, the British government did not provide relief.

Survivors fled the stricken land aboard leaking, creaking 'coffin ships'. Irish refugees swamped towns such as Liverpool, Halifax, Boston, and New York. The famine reduced the population of Ireland by over two million – half dying, the rest emigrating. The population has never returned to pre-famine figures, and a pattern of emigration was established – exporting Irish people, politics, culture, traditions, and sport all over the globe.

FRUSTRATION AND REVOLT

Towards the end of the nineteenth century, the charismatic leader Charles Stewart Parnell came close to winning Home Rule for Ireland, until it was revealed he was having an affair with a married woman and lost support. Nationalist sentiment and resentment continued to grow, though, and in 1905 a political party called Sinn Féin ('We Ourselves') was formed. The Home Rule Act was eventually passed by the House of Commons, but the outbreak of World War I placed it on hold.

During the 1916 Easter Rising, nationalist and socialist insurgents seized several strategic buildings, including Dublin's General Post Office, from where they declared Ireland's independence. The authorities crushed the rising, which lacked widespread support (many Irishmen were fighting alongside the British on the Western Front, believing Home Rule would be granted after the war), but their pitiless execution of the ringleaders reversed public opinion. The fight for independence was reinvigorated.

At the next general election Sinn Féin, led by Éamon de Valera, won by a landslide. The newly elected parliamentarians refused to take their seats in London's House of Commons, and instead set themselves up in Dublin as Dáil Éireann, the new parliament of Ireland.

More than two years of guerrilla warfare followed until the Anglo-Irish Treaty was signed by leading IRA General Michael Collins in December 1921, accepting the partition of Ireland. Six counties in the north were allowed to remain part of the United Kingdom. The other 26 counties had a Catholic majority and became the Irish Free State (Éire), a dominion within the British Empire. Many Irish republicans rejected the treaty and a bitter civil war erupted, claiming over 1,000 lives and lasting until 1923. Nine years later Éamon de Valera came to power, vowing to reinstate the ancient Gaelic language and culture. The

The Liberator

Daniel O'Connell was one of the first Irish Catholics to qualify as a barrister, and went on to secure the repeal of anti-Catholic legislation in 1829, which earned him the sobriquet 'the Liberator'.

26 counties of Éire remained neutral in World War II and formally became an independent republic in 1949.

In Northern Ireland, where Protestants wielded power from Stormont, many Catholics did not recognise the province's legitimacy. The best housing and good jobs in industries such as shipbuilding were almost exclusively the preserve of Protestants, and the Royal Ulster Constabulary was perceived as a sectarian force, breeding huge resentment within impoverished Catholic enclaves. In the late 1960s, civil rights marches against these injustices were violently repressed, unleashing mass rioting. The British Army were sent onto the streets in 1969 and initially welcomed by the minority Catholic communities. Soon, though, the occupying soldiers were seen as siding with the Unionists, and incidents such as Bloody Sunday, when paratroopers shot 28 unarmed civilians, inflamed the conflict.

After three decades of violence, the Good Friday Agreement, signed in 1998, established a framework for a peaceful, self-governing Northern Ireland. In 2005, the IRA declared a permanent ceasefire and decommissioned its weapons, preparing the way for the formation of a new government in May 2007. British troops finally left, and the border between Northern Ireland and the Republic, so long a livid scar, became almost invisible.

In 2002, Ireland was one of the first twelve countries to adopt the euro. With the creation of new industries and huge investment in infrastructure, the 'Celtic Tiger' roared. Then, in the wake of the 2008 global financial crisis, Ireland entered a severe recession. By 2014 the country had emerged from the recession, but the fear since 2016 has been that Brexit will disrupt this fragile peace.

Across Ireland, however, socially progressive politics have blossomed. After a series of scandals involving the church, the youthful population of the Republic has cast aside decades of Catholic-influenced conservatism, and referendums in 2015 and 2018 led to the legalisation of same-sex marriage and abortion.

IMPORTANT DATES

c.500 BC Celts migrate to Britain. Ireland's Iron Age begins.

c.432 St Patrick converts Ireland to Christianity.

1014 Brian Ború, High King of Ireland, defeats the Vikings near Clontarf.

1366 Statutes of Kilkenny forbid English to intermarry or speak Gaelic.

1541 Henry VIII declares himself King of Ireland.

1690 William of Orange defeats England's Catholic King James II at the Battle of the Boyne.

1800–01 Act of Union makes Ireland part of the United Kingdom.

1845–49 The Great Famine; over 1 million people die.

1918–23 Sinn Féin forms Irish parliament in Dublin. The 1921 Anglo-Irish Treaty creates the Irish Free State, sparking civil war.

1949 Having remained neutral in World War II, Éire leaves the British Commonwealth and becomes the Republic of Ireland.

1972 British soldiers shoot 28 demonstrators on 'Bloody Sunday', killing 14. Belfast's parliament is dissolved. Northern Ireland is ruled from London.

1973 The Republic of Ireland joins the EEC (now the European Union).

1998 The Good Friday Agreement is signed in Northern Ireland.

2011 After the collapse of the Fianna Fail government, a coalition government is formed by Fine Gael and Labour. Queen Elizabeth II pays her first visit to Ireland.

2015 The Republic of Ireland legalises same-sex marriage.

2016 Britain votes to leave the EU, raising fears that a hard border will be re-established between the Republic and Northern Ireland.

2017 Power-sharing between Unionists and Republicans in Northern Ireland collapses, leaving the North with no functioning government.

2018 The Republic of Ireland legalises abortion. Michael D. Higgins re-elected as President.

2019 Abortion is decriminalised and same-sex marriage is legalised in NI

2020 Ireland goes into full lockdown on March 27 to stop the spread of the novel coronavirus. The country does considerably well during the pandemic compared to its closest neighbours.

2021 Borders reopen to visitors in July alongside the rest of Europe.

Dublin's Samuel Beckett Bridge

OUT AND ABOUT

The best way to see Ireland is by car, though various package deals or bus tours exist as an alternative. You can see a good deal of the country using public transport, although apart from the main routes, the bus schedules are designed more for locals than tourists.

This book covers the highlights of the Republic and Northern Ireland, starting in Dublin and proceeding clockwise. We cannot describe all the sights – or all the counties – but wherever you go, you'll enjoy Ireland best at an unhurried Irish pace.

DUBLIN

The Republic of Ireland's capital (circa 1.4 million) is the birthplace and muse of many great authors, and an elegant European city with many outstanding examples of eighteenth-century architecture. From its noble avenues and intimate side streets to chic shopping and traditional pubs, **Dublin ❶** is characterised by contrasting moods; a melting pot of old and new where traditional lace still masks modern windows. Amid all the historic monuments, lie museums, colleges, and sporting venues.

O'CONNELL STREET TO ST STEPHEN'S GREEN

The main avenue in Dublin is **O'Connell Street**. Measuring 46m (150ft) across, it has several monuments to Irish history lined along the middle. The Millennium Spire, a

What's in a name?

The city's name comes from the Irish 'Dubh Linn', meaning 'a dark pool'. The alternative Gaelic name, 'Baile Átha Cliath', means 'the town of the hurdle ford'.

395-foot high stainless-steel monument, replaced the nineteenth-century Nelson's Pillar blown up by anti-British rebels in 1966.

O'Connell Street's most famous landmark is the **General Post Office (GPO)**. The GPO served as the insurgents' headquarters during the 1916 Easter Rising and was badly damaged in the fighting. A plaque on the front of the building commemorates the event. The onsite museum, GPO Museum Witness History, documents the 1916 Rising and its aftermath.

Just opposite O'Connell Bridge is the imposing monument honouring 'The Liberator', Daniel O'Connell (1775–1847, see page 19), after whom both the street and bridge are named.

From the bridge, wider than it is long, you can look along the embankments of the **River Liffey**. To the east rises the copper dome of the eighteenth-century **Custom House**. Like many

The General Post Office

buildings along the Liffey, it was badly damaged in the Irish War of Independence (1919–21) and subsequent Civil War (1922–23). Further east lies the shiny new IFSC (Irish Financial Services Centre), gateway to the high-rise Docklands area, with modern apartments and the 2,000-seat Grand Canal Theatre. To the west is the **Ha'penny Bridge**, so-called because that's what it originally cost to cross.

The imposing white building facing College Green on the south side of the River Liffey is a branch of the **Bank of Ireland**, originally home of the Irish parliament in the eighteenth century. The bank moved in when parliament was abolished by the Act of Union in 1801 (see page 19).

Behind the railings at the entrance to **Trinity College** Ⓐ are the statues of two famous alumni – philosopher Edmund Burke and playwright Oliver Goldsmith. Founded by Queen Elizabeth I in 1592, Trinity is a timeless enclave of calm and scholarship in the middle of this bustling city. Until 1793 it was an exclusively Protestant institution, and the Catholic Church forbade Catholics to attend Trinity 'under pain of mortal sin' right up until the late 1960s. Today, TCD, as it is called, is integrated. Students lead informative college tours from a desk at the front porch (June–Sept daily, every 30-40 minutes from 9.45am; Oct–May Fri, Sat, Sun & Mon).

The campus forms a beautiful monument to academia and architecture, and visitors enjoy cobbled walks among trimmed lawns, fine old trees, statues, and stone buildings. You can also enjoy art exhibitions at the Douglas Hyde Gallery, (www.douglashydegallery.com) and the child-friendly Science Gallery (https://dublin.sciencegallery.com).

The greatest treasures are in the vaulted Long Room in the **Old Library** (June–Sept Mon, Tues, Wed, Thurs, Fri & Sat 9am–6pm, Sun 9.30am–6pm; Oct–May Mon, Tues, Wed, Thurs, Fri & Sat

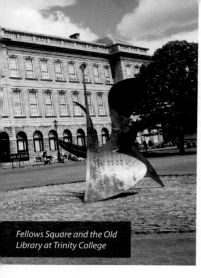

*Fellows Square and the Old
Library at Trinity College*

9.30am–5pm, Sun noon–4.30pm; www.tcd.ie), where double-decker shelving holds thousands of books published prior to 1800, and priceless early manuscripts are displayed in glass cases. In the adjacent Colonnades Gallery, queues of tourists reverently wait for a look at the **Book of Kells**. This 340-page parchment wonder, handwritten and illustrated by monks during the ninth century, contains a Latin version of the New Testament. The beauty of the script – the illumination (the decoration of initial letters and words) – and the bright abstract designs make this the most wonderful treasure to survive from Ireland's Golden Age. The vellum leaves are turned every day to protect them from light and to give visitors a chance to come back for more.

A left turn on leaving Trinity by the main gate brings you to the entrance of **Grafton Street** ⓑ, the main shopping and social artery of the city's southside. More than anywhere else, Grafton Street demonstrates Dublin's knack for seeming to bustle and dawdle at the same time. Buskers entertain passers-by on their way to Brown Thomas, the city's famous high-end department store, and other shopping emporiums, such as the stunning Powerscourt Townhouse Centre, and the Stephen's Green Shopping Centre at the south end.

Examples of Europe's finest Georgian houses can be seen facing **Merrion Square**. The discreet, smart brick houses have Georgian doorways flanked by tall columns and topped by fanlights. No two are alike. In a complex of formal buildings on the west side of the square stands the city's largest eighteenth-century mansion, Leinster House, once home to the dukes of Leinster. Today, **Leinster House** is the seat of the Irish parliament, which consists of the Senate *(Seanad Éireann)* and the Chamber of Deputies (the *Dáil*, pronounced 'doyle'). Just north of here, on Merrion Square West, is the National Gallery.

At the entrance to the **National Gallery of Ireland ⓒ** (Mon 11am–5.30pm, Tues, Wed, Thurs, Fri & Sat 9.45am–5.30pm, Sun 11.30am–5.30pm; permanent collection free, charge for some exhibitions; www.nationalgallery.ie) you will see a statue of George Bernard Shaw, the famous and respected Dubliner known locally as a benefactor of the institution. The gallery has a collection of over 16,300 artworks. Irish artists receive priority, but other nationalities are well represented, such as Dutch, English, Flemish, French, Italian, and Spanish masters, including Fra Angelico, Rubens, Rembrandt, Canaletto, Gainsborough, Goya, Van Gogh, and Renoir.

The main entrance to the **National Museum of Ireland ⓓ** (Tues, Wed, Thurs & Fri 10am–5pm, Sun & Mon 1–5pm; free; www.museum.ie), a Dublin institution showcasing the country's archaeology and history, is reached from Kildare Street. Its collection of antiquities holds several surprises, from Irish bog bodies to exquisite gold ornaments of the Bronze Age. Famous items include the eight-century Ardagh Chalice, the delicate Tara Brooch from the same era and the twelfth-century Shrine of St Patrick's Bell. You can also see ancient Ogham stones and replicas of the greatest carved stone crosses from the early centuries of Christian Ireland.

Dublin is well-endowed with squares and parks, including **St Stephen's Green ⓔ** one of the biggest city squares in Europe. During the eighteenth century the square was almost completely surrounded by elegant town houses. Some survive today, though many conservationists despair at the rapidly declining number. Inside the square is a delightful park with flower gardens and an artificial lake favoured by waterfowl. Among many sculptures and monuments is a memorial to the poet and playwright W.B. Yeats by Henry Moore. Nearby is a bust to commemorate Yeats's friend, Countess Constance Markievicz, who defended the square during the 1916 insurrection, and who was the first woman elected to the British House of Commons. (She declined to take her seat, in line with Sinn Féin's abstentionist policy, but served in the Dáil after Independence.)

Another statue honours the man who paid for landscaping the square: Lord Ardilaun, son of the founder of the Guinness brewery. Some thirsty sightseers might be inspired to find a nearby pub and raise a toast to this stout-hearted benefactor.

MEDIEVAL DUBLIN

Dublin Castle ⑨ (daily 9.45am–5.45pm; www.dublincastle.ie), set on a hill above the original Viking settlement on the south bank of the River Liffey, dates to the thirteenth century, but was mostly rebuilt during the eighteenth century. Over the years it has served as a seat of government, a prison, a courthouse, and occasionally as a fortress under siege. Many visiting heads of state have stayed in the lavish State Apartments.

Just behind the castle is the **Chester Beatty Library** ⑨ (Tues, Thurs & Fri 9.45am–5.30pm, Wed 9.45am–8pm, Sat 9.45–5.30pm, Sun 12.00–5.30pm; free; www.cbl.ie), home to a collection of priceless manuscripts and miniatures: jade books from China, early Arabic tomes on geography and astronomy, a sampling of Korans, and rare Gospel texts. Around the corner from the castle stands **City Hall**, built in the late eighteenth century in solid, classical style. Downstairs, an exhibition tells the story of the Irish capital.

Dublin has two noteworthy cathedrals, and although it is the official capital of what is a predominantly Catholic country, both belong to the Protestant Church of Ireland.

Christ Church Cathedral  (Mon, Thurs, Fri & Sat 10am–5pm, Sun 1–3pm; entry fee; http://christchurchcathedral.ie) is the older of the two, dating from 1038. One unusual architectural touch is the covered pedestrian bridge over Winetavern Street, which links the church and its Synod Hall. This was built during the Victorian era, but doesn't spoil the overall mood. Otherwise, the cathedral contains Romanesque, Early English, and fine neo-Gothic elements.

The crypt, now displaying many of Christ Church's valuable treasures, runs under the length of the church, and is a surviving remnant from the twelfth century, during which time the cathedral

Christ Church Cathedral

A classic Irish pub in Temple Bar

was expanded by Strongbow (see page 16), whose remains reput-
edly lie buried here (There is some debate about the authenticity
of the Strongbow tomb). You can see the fine statue of a recum-
bent cross-legged knight in full armour upstairs.

If you would like to delve deeper into Viking and medieval
Dublin visit the Synod Hall to see an impressive living history
museum **Dublinia** (Thurs, Fri, Sat & Sun 10am– 5.30pm; www.
dublinia.ie). Actors recreate how Viking and medieval Dubliners
lived and encourage visitors to get involved too. Great for kids
of all ages.

A short walk south from Christ Church Cathedral leads to
Dublin's slightly newer and larger cathedral, **St Patrick's** ❶ (Mar–
Oct Mon, Tues, Wed, Thurs, Fri & Sat 9.30am–5pm, Sun 9–10.30am,
12.30–2.30pm, 4.30–6pm; Nov–Feb Mon, Tues, Wed, Thurs & Fri
9.30am–5pm, Sat 9am–5pm, Sun 9–10.30am, 12.30–2.30pm; www.
stpatrickscathedral.ie), which is dedicated to Ireland's national

saint. It is said that St Patrick himself baptised fifth-century converts at a well on this very site; indeed, a stone slab used for covering the well can be found in the northwest of the cathedral. This church was consecrated in 1192, but the present structure dates mostly from the thirteenth and fourteenth centuries. The cathedral is known for its association with Jonathan Swift, author of *Gulliver's Travels*, who was appointed dean in 1713 and served until his death in 1745. Many Swiftian relics occupy a corner of the north transept, and a simple brass plate in the floor near the entrance marks his grave. Next to this you can see the tomb of his beloved 'Stella'. Above the lintel of the robing room you can read his self-written epitaph, etched in Latin on Kilkenny marble: 'Here lies the body of Jonathan Swift, Doctor of Divinity and Dean of this Cathedral, Where savage indignation can no longer lacerate

TEMPLE BAR

Temple Bar is a network of small streets full of studios, galleries, second-hand bookshops, clothing outlets, and music stores. There are countless restaurants, pubs, and crafts shops. Many Dubliners regard it as a tourist trap, but it has some worthwhile cultural centres.

Project Arts Centre: theatre and avant-garde art gallery.

The Button Factory: nightclub and concert venue.

Irish Film Institute: arthouse cinema with bookshop, café/restaurant, bar, and film archive.

Gallery of Photography: exhibits Irish and international work.

National Photographic Archive: maintains and exhibits historical images of Ireland.

Jam Art Factory: Irish art and design shop.

The Ark: arts and entertainment centre for children.

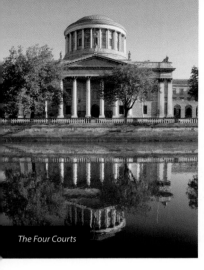
The Four Courts

his heart; Go traveller and imitate if you can, this dedicated and earnest champion of liberty.'

The talented choirboys of St Patrick's Cathedral sing at the services given every day of the week except Saturdays. A joint choir formed from both cathedrals was the first to sing Handel's *Messiah* when the composer was in Dublin in 1742. A copy from the year 1799 can be seen in **Marsh's Library** ❶ (Tues, Wed, Thurs & Fri 9.30am–5pm, Sat 10am–5pm; www.marshlibrary.ie), Ireland's first public library, founded in 1701.

Called the 'Left Bank' by tourist officials, **Temple Bar** ❶ (see page 33) is Dublin's cultural quarter, running from Westmoreland Street to Christ Church Cathedral. With its eighteenth- and nineteenth-century architecture it's not just the cultural quarter of Dublin, but also a land of themed bars and raucous nightclubs. It's best on Saturdays as there is a gourmet food market on Meeting House Square, a book market on Temple Bar Square, and a craft and design market on Cow's Lane.

THE NORTH BANK

The most impressive building located on the north bank of the Liffey is the domed **Four Courts** (originally the Chancery, Common Pleas, Exchequer and King's Bench). This is the magnificent work of James Gandon, the respected eighteenth-century

English-born architect, he also designed Dublin's Custom House. The courthouse was seriously damaged by prolonged shelling during the 1922–23 civil war. After lengthy reconstruction, however, it was fully restored, and justice continues to be dispensed in the Four Courts.

St Michan's Church (Mar–Oct Mon, Tues, Wed, Thurs & Fri 10am–12.45pm, 2–4.30pm, Sat 10am–12.45pm; Nov–Mar Mon, Tues, Wed, Thurs & Fri 12.30–3.30pm, Sat 10am–12.45pm; charge for tours of the crypt) is just around the corner in Church Street. Founded in 1095, it has been rebuilt several times. Among the curiosities is an unusual 'Penitent's Pew', in which sinners had to sit and confess their sins aloud to the whole congregation. In the crypt, wood coffins and mummies can be seen in a remarkable state of preservation. Some of them have been here for about 800 years, saved from deterioration by the dry atmosphere. You can touch the finger of the mummified crusader for good luck.

The last imposing official building to be designed by the architect James Gandon was the **King's Inns ⓛ**, which houses the headquarters of the Irish legal profession. It contains an important law library and a magnificent dining hall, where grand portraits of many judges decorate the walls.

On the north side of Parnell Square is Charlemont House, an attractive eighteenth-century mansion, it is now the site of **Dublin City Gallery The Hugh Lane ⓜ** (Tues, Wed & Thurs 9.45am–6pm, Fri 9.45–5pm, Sat 10am–5pm, Sun 11am–5pm; free; www.hughlane.ie). It includes works from the fine collection of Sir Hugh Lane, whose drowning in the *Lusitania* disaster of 1915 (see page 59) provoked a long legal battle over custody of his paintings. The current agreement assures the Dublin City Gallery three-quarters of the contested legacy, including works by Corot, Courbet, Manet, Monet, and Rousseau. The gallery also houses the Francis Bacon Studio, its contents were transported from London in 1998 and meticulously recreated, along with displays of the famous artist's works.

Next door to the gallery, the **Dublin Writers Museum** Ⓝ (daily 10am–5pm, on some holidays 11am–4.45pm; www.writersmuseum.com) displays photographs, manuscripts and first editions relating to writers such as Swift, Shaw, Yeats, O'Casey, Joyce, Beckett and Behan. At 35 North Great George's Street is the **James Joyce Centre** Ⓞ (Oct–Mar Tues, Wed, Thurs, Fri & Sat 10am–5pm, Sun noon–5pm; Apr–Sept Mon, Tues, Wed, Thurs, Fri & Sat 10am–5pm, Sun noon–5pm; www.jamesjoyce.ie) for Joyce enthusiasts.

BEYOND THE CENTRE

Phoenix Park (www.phoenixpark.ie) provides Dubliners with nearly 3sq miles (8sq km) of beautiful parkland. The perfect way to get around the park is to hire bikes at the main Parkgate St entrance (www.phoenixparkbikes.com). Whizz past Europe's tallest obelisk the Wellington Testimonial and the residence of the President of Ireland, *Áras an Uachtaráin* (guided tours Sat only). Farmleigh House (daily 10am–5pm; www.farmleigh.ie) is a 78-acre (31-hectare) estate with stately home and beautiful gardens that once belonged to the Guinness family. To find out more about the history of the park visit the Phoenix Park Visitor Centre – Ashtown Castle (Nov–Apr Wed, Thurs, Fri, Sat & Sun 9.30am–6pm; May–Oct daily 9.30am–6pm). On the northeast side of the park, **Dublin Zoo** (daily 9.30am–4pm; www.dublinzoo.ie) provides education and diversion; it is noted for breeding lion cubs in captivity and is one of Europe's oldest zoos (1831).

In Kilmainham, a stone tower gate guards the grounds of the **Royal Hospital**, which was a home for army pensioners. Now it is the **Irish Museum of Modern Art** (Tue, Thurs, Fri & Sat 10am–5.30pm, Wed 11.30am–5.30pm, Sun noon–5:30pm; free;

www.imma.ie) and holds first-class temporary exhibitions.

The forbidding **Kilmainham Gaol** (Oct–Mar daily 9:30am–5:30pm; April– May daily 9am–6pm; June–Sept 9:30am–6pm; entry by guided tour only, book in advance: www.kilmainham-gaolmuseum.ie) has been carefully restored. Many heroes of Irish nationalism lived and died as prisoners here. The central cellblock shows exhibits from Ireland's stormy history.

Many make their way to the city's biggest commercial enterprise, the **Guinness Brewery**, situated at St James' Gate since 1759. Its dark, full-bodied stout is world-renowned. Visitors to its award-winning **Storehouse** (Sun, Mon, Tues, Wed & Thurs 10am–5pm, Fri & Sat 10am–7pm; www.guinness-storehouse.com) get an entertaining explanation of how the brew is made and a sample of the finished product.

The Drawing Room in Malahide Castle

DUBLIN DAYTRIPS

NORTH OF DUBLIN

The northeastern part of Dublin Bay, **Howth peninsula,** makes an appealing starting point for those wishing to venture out of Dublin. From the vantage point of the 170-m (560-ft) Hill of Howth, you can survey the bay and the sea. Howth Harbour, on the north side of the peninsula, is a fishing port and haven for pleasure boats. From here you can see and visit Ireland's Eye (www.islandferries. net), an islet 1.5km (1 mile) offshore that is popular with birds and bird-watchers.

Malahide, a small resort town, is best known for its **castle** (daily 9.30am–5.30pm; www.malahidecastleandgardens. ie), a two-turreted medieval pile. The spirit of the Talbot family, who resided here for 791 years, still pervades. Their story is explained in an interpretive centre. Part of the National Portrait Collection is housed here and the castle's rooms, including a medieval great hall, are fully furnished. The Talbot Botanic Gardens were started in 1948, and contain 5,000 labelled species on 250 acres, and seven glasshouses. It is the most important botanic collection after London's Kew Gardens.

Drogheda ❷, a small industrial town, straddles the River Boyne near the site of the 1690 battle in which King

---

Winter lottery

The overwhelming demand to see Newgrange during the winter solstice has forced Irish Heritage to hold a lottery. Visitors can sign up in the welcome centre. Or you can email your postal address and contact phone number to brunaboinne@opw.ie and they'll enter your name. From an average 35,000 entries, 50 names are chosen.

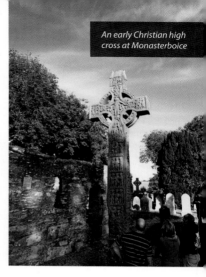

James II failed to recover the British crown (see page 19). This medieval city was surrounded by a wall with 10 gates – you can still drive through the thirteenth-century **St Lawrence's Gate**, with its two towers. In the town centre **St Peter's Church** has been dedicated to St Oliver Plunkett (1628–81), the Archbishop of Armagh who was executed by the British for an alleged papist plot. Several relics of the local saint are displayed in the church, including the actual door of his cell at Newgate Prison and, most amazing of all, his head, which is embalmed and kept in a gold case in a side altar.

About 10km (6 miles) to the northwest is **Monasterboice** (St Buite's Abbey), one of Ireland's numerous ancient monastic settlements. Over it stands the jagged top of what is thought to have been the tallest round tower in Ireland, 34m (110ft) high. Along with the remains of two ruined churches there are three important examples of early Christian high crosses, with intricately carved figures.

A high medieval gatehouse guards the approach to **Old Mellifont Abbey** (daily 24 hours; www.heritageireland.ie), Ireland's most important early Cistercian monastery. Among the buildings stand the remains of a large church and the Lavabo, a graceful octagonal building of which only four sides remain. The abbey is set in peaceful and verdant country.

The Neolithic tomb at Newgrange

Newgrange ❸ (Brú na Boinne Visitor Centre; daily Feb–Apr and Oct 9.30am–5.30pm; May and late-Sept 9am–6.30pm; June–early Sept 9am–7pm; Nov–Jan 9am–5pm; www.newgrange.com/www.heritageireland.ie), a large Neolithic tomb in the Boyne Valley, looks like a man-made hilltop, but is in fact an amazing feat of prehistoric engineering – one of Europe's best examples of a passage grave. The narrow tunnel leading to the central shrine is positioned to let the sun shine in on the shortest day of the year, 21 December. The 19-m (62-ft) tunnel is just high and wide enough to walk through at a crouch. At its end you can stand in the circular vault and look up at the ceiling to see the remarkable 4,000-year-old technique used in its construction.

Carvings in spiral, circular and diamond designs decorate the stones in the inner sanctum and entrance. Outside, a dozen large, upright stones, about a third the original number, form a protective circle. Access is by guided tour only; numbers are limited, so arrive early (last tours 90 min before closing). There are two more Neolithic tumuli at Knowth and Dowth.

The scribes and artists of the monastery at **Kells** in County Meath, produced the nation's most beautiful book, now on display at Trinity College in Dublin (see page 27). The town of Kells has grown up around the monastic settlement, and there is a fine Celtic cross standing at the main traffic junction. In the churchyard are several other stone crosses and a 30-m (100-ft) high round tower.

As its name indicates, **Trim** ❹ is a well-kept, tidy town, but the English name is derived from the Irish *Baile Átha Trium*, which means 'the town of the Elder Tree Ford'. Trim claims it has Ireland's largest medieval **castle** (mid-Feb–Oct daily 10am–5pm; Nov–mid-Feb Sat & Sun 9am–5pm; www.heritageireland.ie), once a Norman stronghold. Vast it is, but time has left only the bare bones. The Dublin Gate in the south once contained a prison. Across the river, the Yellow Steeple was part of an Augustinian abbey established in the thirteenth century; the tower was blown up to keep it out of Cromwell's hands.

WEST OF DUBLIN

County Kildare has some of the greenest pastures in all of Ireland. It's a great area for sports, and there are plenty of historic sites amid the rolling hills. **Maynooth**, a pleasant town with an historic college and the ruins of a twelfth-century castle, was renowned in the nineteenth and twentieth centuries as a training centre for priests.

Ruined monastery

The ruins of an ancient monastery are at the southern end of County Kildare, in the village of Castledermot. Two beautifully carved crosses remain near the portal of a church that could be as much as 1,000 years old. The design of this ruin is repeated in a new church just a few yards behind it.

Founded in 1795, **St Patrick's College** was one of the foremost Catholic seminaries in the world. It is now part of the National University of Ireland.

On the edge of Celbridge village, **Castletown House** ❺ (Wed–Sun 10am–5pm West Wing Exhibition space and Courtyard Café only; www.castletownhouse.ie) stands at the end of a long avenue of trees. This vast stately home, in Palladian style, was erected in 1722 for the speaker of the Irish House of Commons, William Conolly, and has been restored and refurnished with eighteenth-century antiques and paintings. Conolly's widow ordered the construction of a monstrous obelisk 5km (3 miles) from the house. Known as Conolly's Folly, it was erected to provide jobs for local workers suffering from the famine of 1740–41.

The administrative centre of the county, **Naas** (the Irish *Nás na Ríogh* means 'Assembly Place of the Kings') has an important racecourse. So does nearby Punchestown, but the capital of horse racing and breeding is the **Curragh** ❻, a 2,000 hectare stretch of flat racing turf, grazed by sheep and used for exercise gallops by many training stables. It's a shock to come upon a modern grandstand – site of the Irish Sweeps Derby – in the middle of this vast plain.

Many winners of the biggest races are born near Kildare Town at the **National Stud** Farm (daily 10am–6pm; www.irishnationalstud. ie). Here thoroughbreds live in a first-class 'horse resort'. Beside the Irish Horse Museum, there is an immaculate **Japanese Garden** – once a bog, now a world of tidy shrubs and trees. There's even a lotus pond, teahouse and red wooden bridge.

The town of **Kildare** is also remembered for the double monastery (monks and nuns) founded there by fifth-century St Brigid. Though Vikings and other invaders damaged the buildings quite badly, the shape of the nineteenth-century **cathedral** features thirteenth-century elements. Nearby is an ancient round tower still in very good shape, with stairs all the way to the top. Another attraction is Kildare Village (daily 10am–7pm; www.kildarevillage.com) for chic outlet shopping.

SOUTH OF DUBLIN

Dún Laoghaire ❼ (pronounced Dunleary), just south of Dublin, a former international port, is Ireland's leading yachting centre, with several clubs. The piers at the harbour are 2km (1 mile) long, leaving plenty of space for the huge fleet of pleasure boats that dock here. Construction of the harbour was a great feat of nineteenth-century engineering – and remains impressive. The newest addition to the Dún Laoghaire skyline is the ship prow-like Lexicon Library and Cultural Centre (http://libraries.dlrcoco.ie), with fine views of Dublin Bay from the top floor, situated a few short steps from the National Maritime Museum (daily 11am–5pm; www.mariner.ie).

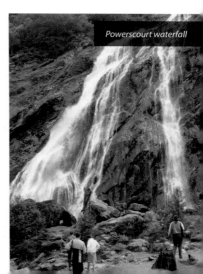

Powerscourt waterfall

Around 1.5km (1 mile) south at **Sandycove** is an eighteenth-century Martello tower, built as part of Dublin's coastal defences designed to keep Napoleon at bay. James Joyce stayed here, and the tower features in the opening of his novel *Ulysses*. It now houses the **James Joyce Tower and Museum** (daily 10am–4pm, to 6pm Apr–Oct; free; www.jamesjoycetower.com). A second Martello tower can be seen on Dalkey Island (boat trips daily www.kentheferryman.com).

Just across the border in County Wicklow, the 'Garden of Ireland', the popular resort of **Bray** (www.bray.ie) has a 2km (1 mile) sand-and-shingle beach backed by an esplanade. The 7km-Cliff Walk along the Bray Head headland leads to Greystones, a postcard-pretty coastal town.

West of Bray, near Enniskerry, is the grand estate of **Powerscourt** ❽ (daily 9.30am–5.30pm or dusk in winter; www.powerscourt.ie). Covering 20 hectares (47 acres) of glorious countryside and gardens, the estate has an eighteenth-century, 100-room mansion. at its centre, which was damaged in a fire in 1974. Today, it contains an exhibition devoted to the history of the estate. From the house, disciplined terraces descend to a lake with a fountain in the middle. The garden centre is also worth a visit, as is the Powerscourt Waterfall, 5km (3 miles) south of the house. There is an Avoca café for a quick bite to eat.

In a narrow, wooded valley with two lakes stand the evocative ruins of the ancient monastic settlement of **Glendalough** ❾ (mid-Mar–mid-Oct 9.30am–6pm; mid-Oct–mid-Mar 9.30am–5pm;

THE WICKLOW WAY

You'll need the better part of a week to see all the Wicklow Way, an ancient path stretching 132km (82 miles) from the suburbs of Dublin to the Wexford border town of Clonegal. A shorter option is the popular stretch from Knockree, 5km (3 miles) west of Enniskerry, to Glendalough. It'll take you about three days to cover this area, and you'll be able to step foot on the highest point of the trail – White Hill, from which on a clear day you can see the mountains in Wales.

Re-enactments at the Irish National Heritage Park

www.glendalough.ie). The hermit St Kevin founded the monastery here in the sixth century, evidently inspired by the breathtaking, remote scenery. He planned it as a small, contemplative institution, but as its fame spread far and wide, Glendalough of the Seven Churches became an important monastic centre, until 1398, when it was destroyed by Anglo-Normans.

The surviving buildings date from the eighth and twelfth centuries. The most famous is the **round tower**, which is 34m (112ft) high and 16m (52ft) in circumference at the base. This was the place to sit out any sieges; its doorway is built 3.5m (11ft) above the ground – enough to discourage even Vikings from invading. Remnants of a cathedral, stone churches, and decorated crosses can also be seen, and the original gateway to the settlement, the only one of its kind in Ireland, is still standing. Inside, on the right, a cross-inscribed stone may have marked the limit of the sanctuary granted to those who took refuge within the monastery. In the graveyard, tombstones dating back hundreds of years sit next to more recent graves.

In **Avondale**, you can visit **Avondale House and Gardens** (Easter–Oct Tue–Sun 11am–4pm; hours vary; www.heritage island.com), the home of the great nineteenth-century Irish leader, Charles Stewart Parnell. The Georgian house is set in 202 hectares (500 acres) of forest park, making it an ideal destination

> ### Mudflat harbour
>
> In the ninth century Wexford was called *Waesfjord*, meaning 'the harbour of the mudflats'. At low tide, when the bay empties like a sink, the original name still seems appropriate.

for walkers. **Russborough House** (parklands daily 9am–6pm; house closed Jan–Feb; www.russborough.ie), near Blessington, is an eighteenth-century Palladian mansion, reputed to be the longest house in Ireland at 210m (700ft). It houses a wonderful collection of art and antiques, including works by Goya, Gainsborough, and Reynolds. The magnificent views across the ornamental lake towards the Wicklow Mountains are among the best in Ireland.

THE SOUTHEAST

Over the whole year, the southeast enjoys up to an hour more sunshine a day than other parts of Ireland – perfect for seeing and enjoying the region's magical mountains, pastures, rivers, beautiful beaches, and delightful old towns.

Enniscorthy (the Irish *Inis Coirthe* means Rock Island) is a colourful inland port on the River Slaney, which is navigable from here to Wexford. High above the steep streets of the town, Vinegar Hill is a good vantage point for viewing the countryside. It was the scene of the last battle of the 1798 United Irishmen Rebellion, during which British General Lake overwhelmed the Wexford rebels armed with pitchforks and pikes. **Enniscorthy Castle** (Mon–Fri 9.30am–5pm, Sat–Sun noon–5pm; www.enniscorthycastle.ie), in the centre of town, is an imposing Norman keep, rebuilt during the sixteenth century. It reopened in 2011 after a major renovation, and is benefitting from its resemblance to Harry Potter's school, Hogwarts.

WEXFORD

Wexford, the county seat, 24km (15 miles) south of Enniscorthy, was one of the first Viking settlements in Ireland. A few ancient monuments survive and are well signposted, with informative plaques explaining local legends.

The **Irish National Heritage Park** ❿ (Nov–Feb daily 9.30am–5pm; Mar–Jun daily 9.30am–5.30; Jul–Aug daily 9.30am–6.30pm; Sept–Oct daily 9.30–5.30; irishheritage.ie) in Ferrycarrig, north of the town, contains a collection of life-size replicas of ancient dwellings, burial sites, old monastic settlements and fortifications, from early Irish man to the twelfth century. The Irish Agricultural Museum and Johnstown Castle Gardens (daily 9am–4.30pm) is a magnificent spot for a picnic in the lakeside gardens, designed by Daniel Robertson who also designed Powerscourt Gardens in Co Wicklow.

In October, the Wexford Opera Festival (www.wexfordopera.com) attracts performers and fans from around the world. Southeast of the town, the resort of **Rosslare** has a 10km- (6 mile-) crescent of beach. At Rosslare Harbour, car ferries arrive from and depart for Fishguard, Pembroke, Roscoff and Cherbourg.

The tip of the **Hook peninsula** has the 800-year-old Hook Lighthouse (http://hookheritage.ie). A warning light has been kept burning

Waterford crystal in the making

at Hook Head for the past 1,500 years. For fans of the supernatural, a visit to **Loftus Hall** (http://loftushall.ie), Ireland's most haunted house, is a must-do.

The Norse established ports in Dublin and Wexford, but it somehow never occurred to them to found permanent settlements inland. It was the Normans who moved 32km (20 miles) up the estuary to build **New Ross** ⑪, a sizeable town and still an important inland port. By the riverbank, you will see the tall masts of the Dunbrody Famine Ship (daily 9–6pm; www.dunbrody.com), a full-scale replica of a sailing ship built in 1845 to transport emigrants to North America.

The isolated hamlet of **Dunganstown**, near New Ross, was the birthplace of US President John F. Kennedy's great grandfather. The Kennedy Homestead (daily 9.30pm–5.30pm; www.kennedyhome stead.ie) is a unique cultural museum showcasing the history of the Kennedy family. The assassinated president was much admired in Ireland and a group of Irish-Americans and the Irish government later created the **John F. Kennedy Arboretum** (Oct–Mar daily 10am–5pm; April–Sept daily 10am–6.30pm; www.heritageireland. ie) above Dunganstown.

WATERFORD

Waterford ⑫ is a largely Georgian port, 29km (18 miles) from the open sea. From the far side of the River Suir, its long quayside presents a pretty image. Founded in the ninth century, the town did not gain a charter until 1205, granted by King John. The heritage centre has ancient relics from the Norse and Norman settlements and audiovisual displays. Municipal mementos, including Waterford's important collection of medieval charters, are preserved inside **Reginald's Tower**, the city's most venerable building (Jan–start of March Wed, Thurs, Fri, Sat & Sun 9.30am–5pm; end of March–December daily 9.30am–5.30pm). The walls of this giant circular fortification, 3m- (10ft-) thick and about 24m- (80ft-) tall, have survived many sieges since being erected in 1003.

Among other attractions are the Garter Lane Arts Centre (www.garterlane.ie), a lively venue in a converted town house; the Mall, an elegant Georgian street beginning at the Quay; and Waterford City Hall, built in the 1780s, which has many fine features, including two small theatres and a Council

Cahir Castle

Chamber illuminated by a splendid chandelier made from the famous **Waterford crystal**.

The golden age of Waterford crystal ran from 1783 to 1851. After a century-long lapse, production resumed, only to cease again in 2009. The skills of lowing and cutting lead crystal continue to be demonstrated in the **Waterford Crystal Visitor Centre on the Mall** (factory tour Jan–Feb Mon, Tues, Wed, Thurs & Fri 9.30am–3.15pm; Mar daily 9.30am–3.15pm; Apr–Oct daily 9.30am–4.15pm; Nov–Dec Mon, Tues, Wed, Thurs & Fri 9.30am–3.15pm; www.waterfordvisitorcentre.com).

In **Lismore** ⑬, at the western edge of the county, the **Lismore Experience**, another educational multimedia show, tells the history of this small town founded in the seventh century by St Carthage. Also, **Ormond Castle** in Carrick-on-Suir, Co Tipperary, is the finest Elizabethan manor house in Ireland, now restored to its sixteenth-century glory.

Counties **Kilkenny** and **Tipperary** both feature stunning scenery and imposing ruins. Tipperary was home of the kings of Munster; Kilkenny entered history as the ancient Kingdom of Ossory. The main town in County Tipperary is **Clonmel**, where parts of the fourteenth-century walls can still be seen. The turreted West Gate was rebuilt in 1831 on the site of an original gate. Tipperary Museum of Hidden History (Tue, Wed, Thurs, Fri, & Sat 10am–1pm, 2–3.45pm) on Mick Delahunty Square is well worth a visit.

The name of the town of **Cahir** is a short version of the Irish for 'Fortress of the Dun Abounding in Fish'. Its setting, on the River Suir, is both attractive and strategic. The seemingly impregnable **Cahir Castle** (31 Oct–28 Feb daily 9.30am–4.30pm; seasonal opening times; www.heritageireland.ie) guards the crucial crossing. Built on the river's lovely islet – a site fortified since the third century – the present castle dates from the fifteenth century. It's in a fine state of restoration, and guided tours point out military details, such as musket slits, a portcullis and a cannonball embedded high in one of the walls. While you're in Cahir, take a look at **Swiss Cottage** (Apr–Oct daily 10am–6pm; www.heritageireland.ie), an early nineteenth-century romantic cottage, in the bright Regency style. It has been fully restored right down to the thatched roof and original French wallpaper.

CASHEL

In **Cashel** ⑭, Co Tipperary, monastic ruins crown an imposing hilltop. The **Rock of Cashel** (Daily 9am–3.45pm; www.heritage ireland.ie), is a 61m- (200ft-) high outcrop of limestone, where the kings of Munster had their headquarters from the fourth to the twelfth centuries. St Patrick visited in 450 and baptised King Aengus and his brothers. In 1101 ecclesiastical authorities built an Irish-Romanesque church here. **Cormac's Chapel** (consecrated in 1134) is unique in that it was built by Irish monks who interpreted architectural styles they had studied in Europe. It features a steeply pitched stone roof, rows of blank arches and two oddly positioned towers. Stone-carvings of beasts and abstract designs decorate the doorway and arches.

The chapel is dwarfed by the **cathedral** that abuts it. This structure, dating from the thirteenth century, has thick and well-preserved walls, but the roof collapsed during the eighteenth century. On the positive side, the resulting hole lets the sunlight stream in, helping to clarify the many architectural details, as well as the exquisite medieval stone-carvings.

Inside the entrance, St Patrick's Cross is one of the oldest crosses in Ireland, and it looks like it – the sculptures on both sides are very weather-beaten. The cross rises up from the 'Coronation Stone', said to have been a pagan sacrificial altar.

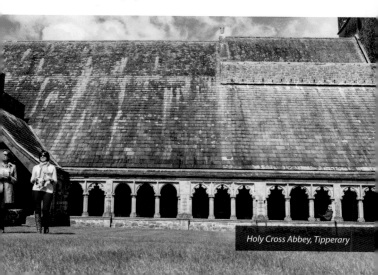

Holy Cross Abbey, Tipperary

It was in the lively market town of **Thurles**, in 1174, that the Irish forces defeated the Anglo-Norman army led by Strongbow (see page 16). Seven hundred years later, the town saw the birth of the Gaelic Athletic Association (GAA), now an amateur sports organisation with 500,000 members worldwide. The Lár na Páirce GAA Museum (Mon, Tues, Wed, Thurs & Sat 10am–5.30pm; http://larnapairce.ie) tells the story of Gaelic games. The most conspicuous landmark of the town, the Catholic Cathedral, was built in a nineteenth-century version of the Romanesque style. The square bell tower, 38m (125ft) high, can be seen for miles around.

On the west bank of the River Suir, 6km (4 miles) south of Thurles is the Cistercian **Holy Cross Abbey**. Construction of the church here, which is still in use, started in Romanesque style, but slowly evolved into Gothic. The solid white walls, enhanced by window-tracery, reach up to a perfectly restored fifteenth-century ceiling. A triple-arched recess contains seats of honour carved from jet-black marble and decorated with ancient coats of arms. Another detail is the night stairs, down which the monks stumbled from their sleeping quarters at 2am to chant matins. One of the bells in the tower was cast in the early thirteenth century, making it Ireland's oldest.

KILKENNY

Kilkenny ⑮ has many historic buildings and an attractive town centre. It's a somewhat arty county which is full of surprises – not least its enormous medieval castle – and a river to boot. This was the capital of the old Kingdom of Ossory, a relatively small realm in pre-Norman Ireland.

Parliament, which convened here in 1366, passed the notorious but ineffectual Statutes of Kilkenny, with the aim of segregating the Irish from the Anglo-Normans (in those days intermarriage was seen as high treason). In the seventeenth century an independent Irish parliament met here for several years. Oliver Cromwell took the town for the English in 1650, suffering heavy losses in the process.

The Irish *Cill Choinnigh* means St Canice's church; **St Canice's Cathedral**, built in the thirteenth century, is on the original site of the church, which gave the town its name. Though Cromwell's rampaging troops badly damaged the building, it has since been restored to an admirable state. Alongside it is a round tower.

Kilkenny Castle (Oct–Mar daily 9:30am–5pm; Apr–Sept daily 9:30am–5:30pm; www.kilkennycastle.ie) was built in the thirteenth century to replace the primitive fortress erected by Strongbow. The Butler family, one of the great Anglo-Norman dynasties, held the castle until 1935, but today it is owned by the Irish state. The ornate Georgian stable of the Castle Yard houses the headquarters of the Design and Crafts Council Ireland (www.dccoi.ie) and the National Craft Gallery (www.ndcg.ie). Kilkenny was at the forefront of the revival of traditional handicrafts and innovative design in Ireland, and the 'craft trail' (brochures available locally) is well worth following.

Kilkenny is packed with bright shops. In the High Street, the Tholsel (city hall), dating from the eighteenth century, has an eight-sided

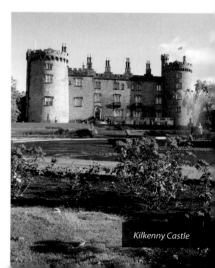

Kilkenny Castle

clock tower. **Rothe House** (http://rothehouse.com), a Tudor town house dating from 1594, has been restored as a museum. The exhibits range from Stone Age tools unearthed locally to medieval relics.

Just outside of **Thomastown** you can visit the partially restored ruins of the Cistercian **Jerpoint Abbey** (Oct daily 9am–5pm; Nov–Dec daily 9am–4pm; seasonal opening times; www.heritageireland.ie). Founded in the mid-twelfth century by the King of Ossory, it had a brief, troubled history before succumbing to the dissolution of the monasteries in 1540. Parts of it retain their Romanesque lines, but the square central tower with its stepped battlements was added during the fifteenth century. Much of the sculptural work in the cloister and church is intact, and you can see larger-than-life carvings of knights and saints, which are inspiring monuments both to those they honour, and to the talented and devoted sculptors who worked here in the Middle Ages.

From Thomastown, make the journey to the picturesque village of **Inistioge**, just 7km (5 miles) away and the location for a famous films such as *The Secret Scripture* starring Rooney Mara, Vanessa Redgrave, Aidan Turner, and Eric Bana and Widow's Peak with Mia Farrow. While you're here, **Woodstock Gardens & Arboretum** are perfect for a scenic woodland walk.

THE SOUTHWEST

CORK

Ireland's largest county marries gently rolling farmland with rugged, stony peninsulas and delightful bays. Enclosed by steep hills, **Cork City** ⑯ has all the facilities of an important commercial and industrial centre, but its atmosphere is unique. The River

Lee divides into two channels to the west of the city centre, leaving the centre on an island connected to its north and south banks by numerous bridges, with seagulls flying overhead and swans gliding by.

The city's name is an anglicisation of *Corcaigh* 'Marshy Place' which is how the area looked in the sixth century when St Finbarr arrived to found a church and school. In the year 820 the Vikings raided marshy

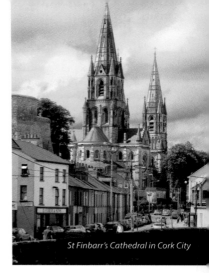

St Finbarr's Cathedral in Cork City

Cork, destroying the institutions and houses. They liked the lay of the land and returned to build their own town on the same site. This destruction and rebuilding repeated like a pattern in the seventeenth century and then again during the Irish War of Independence 1919–21.

The main office for Cork and Kerry Tourism is located on the Grand Parade in Cork and offers free maps of the city centre. Cork's beauty begs slow exploration and one can easily spend the day strolling along its narrow canals and winding streets.

Patrick Street, fondly known as 'Pana' by locals is the wide main street of Cork. It is curved because it was built above a river channel. It makes for great window-shopping anytime and is full of people promenading on Saturday afternoons. A venture across the south channel of the River Lee will take you to **St Finbarr's Cathedral**. The latest version was built in the nineteenth century and follows the lofty French-Gothic style, with arches upon arches. Across the river's north channel on the Christy Ring Bridge and up the hill is St Anne's Church, home to the Shandon Bells and clock tower, fondly known to locals as the 'four-faced liar' due to the apparent disparity in the time being shown on its different sides. Visitors can climb up through the clockwork intricacies and even play a tune on the bells.

Nearby, at Sunday's Well, you can visit the fully restored nineteenth- and early twentieth-century cells of the **Cork City Gaol** (Thurs, Fri, Sat, Sun & Mon 10am–4pm; http://corkcitygaol.com). The same building high above the city was the location of Cork's first radio station, and now hosts a delightfully idiosyncratic radio museum.

COUNTY CORK

Cork is a good centre for excursions. **Blarney Castle** ⑰ (daily 9am–5:30pm; www.blarneycastle.ie) is 8km (5 miles) to the west. Allegedly capable of bestowing the 'gift of the gab' (eloquence), the famous Blarney Stone is kissed by many tourists every day. One of many competing origin stories claims that this is part of the Stone of Scone, gifted to the chieftain Cormac MacCarthy by Robert the Bruce in gratitude for his assistance in the 1314 battle of Bannockburn. To kiss the awkwardly placed stone you need to climb up to the battlement, lie flat on your back, hang on to two iron bars and extend your head backwards.

The castle itself is worth a visit, even if hordes of

Kinsale besieged

Kinsale was under siege in 1601 as Spanish troops, who had sailed to aid the Irish against Queen Elizabeth, were defeated, ultimately sparking the 'flight of the Earls' (the exodus of the Irish nobility) in 1607, and the redistribution of their lands.

Cobh harbour

tourists do besiege it every summer. The formidable keep was built in the middle of the fifteenth century, while the private park, in which the castle stands, includes a grove of ancient yew trees, said to be a site of Druid worship.

Cobh 18, the seaport of Cork city, lies about 24km (15 miles) east of Cork City. It is pronounced 'Cove', which is exactly what it means in Irish.

From Queen Victoria's 1849 visit until 1922, Cobh was called Queenstown. The port is touched by nostalgia – from the tragic traffic of desperate emigrants fleeing the Great Famine for Canada or America to the days of the great transatlantic liners (this was the last port of departure for the ill-fated *Titanic*). **The Queenstown Story** (www.cobh heritage.com) and the **Titanic Experience** (www.titanicexperiencecobh.ie) provide a particular insight into this era. High above the harbour, the spire of the **Cathedral of St Colman** reaches heavenward. Recitals are given in the summer on the cathedral's 47-bell carillon.

In Midleton, to the northeast of Cobh, visit the **Old Midleton Distillery** (www.tours.jamesonwhiskey.com) in a converted whiskey distillery that dates back to the late eighteenth century, which has been occupied by Jameson since 1975. It tells the story of Irish whiskey via an audiovisual presentation, and offers tours and tastings.

The town of **Youghal** (in English pronounced 'Yawl'), east of Midleton, is a resort with 8km (5 miles) of beach and a long seafaring history. The town walls from the Middle Ages can still be seen.

On the site of the main town gate is the **clock tower**, dating from 1776. The high street runs right through it with the structure's four narrow floors and belfry rising above an arched platform over the street. The attractive tower was once a prison, and rebels were hanged from the windows to set an example to the populace.

The most impressive monument in Youghal, **St Mary's Collegiate Church** (Church of Ireland), is thought to have been founded in the fifth century. The present building dates largely from the thirteenth century, and was restored in the nineteenth century. Among the monuments and tombs in the church is one built, in his own honour, by Richard Boyle, an Elizabethan adventurer and the first Earl of Cork. Myrtle Grove, a sixteenth-century house near the churchyard entrance, was briefly home to Sir Walter Raleigh. The Heritage Centre (www.youghal.ie) on the quayside runs frequent guided tours.

Steep hills shelter the seaport of **Kinsale ⑲**, about 29km (18 miles) south of Cork. Its wide, sheltered harbour is a joy to sailors and sightseers alike. Kinsale is renowned for its restaurants, which are among the best in southwest Ireland.

Today, the **harbour** is used by fishing boats, dinghies, and yachts. Ashore are fortifications including the classic star-shaped **Charles Fort** (daily Nov–mid-Mar 10am–5pm; mid-Mar–Oct 10am–6pm; www.heritageireland.ie), the Norman church of St Multose, a museum housing Edward III's first town charter, and the **Desmond Castle International Museum of Wine**.

Migratory birds flock to the **Old Head** of Kinsale, 16km (10 miles) beyond the town. A modern lighthouse here is the successor to a beacon dating back to pre-Christian times. It was off the Old Head that a German submarine torpedoed the world-famous liner, the *Lusitania*, on 7 May 1915, resulting in the loss of 1,500 lives. The inquest into the disaster was held in the Kinsale Court House.

Clonakilty, another coastal town situated between Kinsale and Bantry, is home to the **West Cork Model Railway Village** (daily 11am–5pm; www.modelvillage.ie), which depicts the area's six towns, with a working model of the defunct West Cork Railway.

The town of **Bantry** nestles between steep green hills and a tranquil bay. The main sight is Bantry House (Apr–Oct daily 10am–5pm; Apr–May and Sept–Oct Mon garden only; www.bantryhouse.com), a part-Georgian, part-Victorian stately home full of tapestries, paintings and furnishing and set in sub-tropical gardens.

The Old Head of Kinsale

Heading counter-clockwise around the bay from Bantry, the highway weaves through more rocky hills until it descends upon **Glengarriff** ⑳, where the beauty of the setting and the pleasant climate account for its year-round popularity.

Boat trips (www.bluepoolferry.com; www.harbourqueenferry.com) touted by traditional boatmen in Glengarriff cruise past Seal Island, and you can opt to land on **Garnish Island** (Apr–Oct daily times vary; www.garnishisland.com) a 15-hectare (37-acre) garden. The flora comes from five continents, and the centrepiece is a walled **Italian garden**, surrounding a pool, with the gentle air of a paradisiacal perfume factory. Until 1910, Garinish was a bleak military outpost. From the top of the Martello tower, sentries once kept a lookout for Napoleonic invasion fleets; today, you can survey the luxuriant hills around the bay.

COUNTY KERRY

By any standard this is a spectacular part of the world: the Atlantic in all its moods, lakes designed for lovers or poets, and steep, evergreen mountains. **Killarney** ㉑ is a good base from which to explore the area. Seeing the sights here can be accomplished in many ways – by car, coach, bicycle, boat or even by 'jaunting car' – a horse-drawn rig driven by a *jarvey* (guide) who knows the territory and how to tell a story.

It is best to visit the **Gap of Dunloe** on a fully organised excursion, usually a half-day trip. The Gap, a wild gorge 6km (4 miles) long, can be traversed on a pony, in a pony trap or on foot. Sound effects underline the weirdness of the eerie rock-strewn scenery as echoes bounce off the mountains – **MacGillycuddy's Reeks** in the west (the highest range in Ireland), and to the east, **Purple Mountain**. The long trek leads to the shore of the Upper Lake, where the tour continues by boat to Ross Castle. The scenery around the lakes – thick forests, stark crags and enchanted islands

– could not be more romantic, but there's adventure, too: the **rapids** at Old Weir Bridge.

Muckross Abbey is a friary dating from the fifteenth century with a massive square tower, a cloister with Gothic arches on two sides, Norman or Romanesque on the others and an old, weathered yew tree. **Muckross House** (Jun–Aug daily 9.30am–6pm; Sept–Oct daily 9.30am–5.30pm; Nov–Dec daily 9.30am–5pm; www.muckross-house.ie), which contains exhibits of Kerry crafts and folklore, is surrounded by outstanding gardens. Muckross Traditional Farms (same hours and website) is an enjoyable outdoor attraction recreating traditional farming methods and way of life in the 1930s.

RING OF KERRY

The **Ring of Kerry** ㉒ may well be the most sensational 180km (112 miles) you have ever driven. The ring is a circular route around a coast of rugged cliffs and the enthralling seascapes. This round-trip can be made in either direction, but here we proceed clockwise. Set aside a whole day to really make the most of it.

Leaving Killarney, the road goes past lush lakeland. **Kenmare** is famous for lacemaking and the fish that fill the estuary. North of the small resort of Castlecove, 3km (2 miles) off the main road, are the ruins of **Staigue Fort**. A 2,500-year-old stronghold and one of Ireland's main archaeological wonders, this almost circular structure measures about 27m (90ft) across with a 6m- (18ft-) high wall.

Near Caherdaniel, **Derrynane House**, the home of Daniel O'Connell (see page 19), has been fully restored and is now a museum (opening hours vary; www.derrynanehouse.ie). Game fishing lures visitors to Waterville, as well as the scenery nearby: stark grey glaciated mountains on one side of the road, green fields and the sea on the other.

A bridge connects **Valentia Island**, with its high slate cliffs, to the mainland at Portmagee. The island was the European terminus of the first transatlantic cable (1866), making possible telegraphic contact with America.

Off Valentia, the Skelligs Islands rise abruptly from the ocean, shrouded with mystery and birds. Skellig Michael and its monastic ruins, a UNESCO World Heritage Site, provided the setting for scenes in two Star Wars films (*The Force Awakens* and *The Last Jedi*). Find out more at the Skelligs Heritage Centre (www.skelligexperience.com)

Crag Cave

To the east of Tralee, the town of Castleisland is the location of the Crag Cave (Jan–Mid Mar Fri, Sat & Sun 10am–6pm; March–Oct daily 10am–6pm; Nov–Dec Wed, Thurs, Fri & Sat 10am–6pm; www.cragcave.com). Nearly 4km (2.5 miles) long and bristling with stalagmites and stalactites, this is one of the best show caves in Ireland.

or take a boat to the islands (http://skelligislands.com).

On the north shore of the peninsula, hills plunge to sea level and cliffs complete the descent. **Dingle Bay** seems startlingly wide and the Dingle Peninsula looks like another country.

From Glenbeigh to Killorglin, the head of the bay is almost totally protected from the rough sea by huge sandbars extending from either shore. **Rossbeigh Strand**, with its 6km (4 miles) of golden sand, is a dream beach.

Slea Head on the Dingle Peninsula

The last town on the ring, **Killorglin**, saves all its energy for three days in August and a boisterous pagan pageant called the Puck Fair (http://puckfair.ie), during which time a mountain goat presides over round-the-clock festivities. To the north, **Tralee ㉓**, the administrative centre of County Kerry, owes its fame to the songwriter William Mulchinock (1820–64). *The Rose of Tralee* and its author are honoured in a monument in the town park. During Tralee's annual festival in late August, women of Irish descent from many countries compete in a beauty contest, and the winner is crowned Rose of Tralee (www.roseoftralee.ie).

Kerry County Museum (daily 10am–5pm; www.kerrymuseum. ie) in Tralee offers three experiences all in one. Kerry in Colour is an audiovisual presentation of the splendours of Kerry; the County Museum details Kerry's history since 5000 BC; and the Geraldine Experience reconstructs life in medieval Tralee.

Tralee is the principal gateway to the **Dingle Peninsula**, a long, dramatic finger pointing some 48km (30 miles) into the Atlantic Ocean. On the south shore, amidst rocky coves, a sand-bar grows into an arc of beach jutting more than halfway across the bay. **Inch Strand's** 6km (4 miles) of sand slide gently into the sea. Behind the bathers, archaeologists putter about the dunes, where inhabitants of prehistoric ages left meaningful clues about their way of life.

The small fishing port and resort of **Dingle** ㉔ (officially known as *An Daingean*, the name to look for on signposts) claims to be the most westerly town in Europe. From here to land's end all the hamlets are Irish-speaking parts of the *Gaeltacht* (see page 123), where folklore and traditional language are still preserved. This is rugged farming country, where old stone walls

King John's Castle in Limerick

are overgrown with shrubs, thick hedges divide skimpy parcels of land into fields and hardy sheep graze on even the most precipitous of hills.

The western part of the peninsula is rich territory for archaeologists. In one area, the Fahan group alone consists of an astonishing 400 *clocháns* (beehive-shaped stone huts), along with forts and other ancient structures. For a spectacular panorama, drive up the **Conor Pass** (at an altitude of 460m/1,500ft) and see the sea out to the north and south, and mountains and lakes on the east and west sides. In this part of the world you're isolated from everything but the wild fuchsia and heather beside the road.

THE WEST

LIMERICK AND CLARE

By the time the waters of the River Shannon have reached **Limerick** ㉕ in the west, they have flowed over 274km (170 miles) across all terrains, from narrow streams and swirling rapids to lakes and lochs. After Limerick they still have another 97km (60 miles) to travel through the estuary to the open Atlantic.

Limerick's position at the meeting of the river and its tidal waters assured the city experienced a long and often violent history. The Danes were first on the scene. Their belligerence provoked repeated attacks by the native Irish, who finally drove them out.

The Anglo-Normans in turn captured *Luimneach* – in English 'Bare Spot'. King John visited in 1210 and ordered the construction of a bridge and **King John's Castle** (daily 10am–5pm; www.kingjohnscastle.com), which still survive and have been extensively renovated. A riverside footpath runs from the Tourist Office on Arthur's Quay to the castle, passing the Hunt Museum and St Mary's Cathedral en route. The city endured its most memorable siege after the **Battle of the Boyne** (1690), when Irish supporters of James II (see page 19) retreated to Limerick, pursued by William of Orange. They lost, but the Treaty of Limerick allowed them to leave with honour and guaranteed the Irish freedom of religion. This was repudiated by the English Parliament, so today Limerick carries the title of 'City of the Violated Treaty'.

The 850-year-old **St Mary's Cathedral** (guided tours; www.saint maryscathedral.ie) has an arched Irish-Romanesque west door, while fifteenth-century carved misericords under the choir seats show free-ranging imagination, with representations of angels, animals, and other figures in relief. The waterfront Custom House is now the **Hunt Museum** (Tues. Wed, Thurs, Fri & Sat 10am–5pm, Sun 11am–5pm; www. huntmuseum.com), housing an outstanding collection of Celtic and medieval treasures and a selection of twentieth-century Irish and European art, including works by Picasso and Renoir.

Shannon Airport reinforces Limerick's historic role as a centre of commerce. The airport opened in 1945, making its mark before fast, non-stop transatlantic travel became common. Waiting passengers were offered the new

The extraordinary landscape of the Burren

and rather exclusive opportunity to buy luxury goods exempt from tax. Thus, the world's first duty-free shop expanded and became a shopping centre.

Bunratty Castle ㉖ (Thurs, Fri, Sat & Sun, 9am–5.30pm; www.shannonheritage.com) is a busy tourist attraction about 5km (3 miles) from the airport. At night actors in period costume recreate medieval banquets for visitors.

Barren Burren

A frustrated general serving under Oliver Cromwell famously condemned the desolate Burren as having 'not enough wood to hang a man, not enough water to drown him, not enough clay to cover his corpse'.

A favourite attraction at Bunratty is the **Folk Park** (same hours as the castle) containing replicas of typical old houses of the Shannon region. The peat fires are kept burning, as if the people had just stepped out to milk a cow or catch a fish.

Ennis, the county town of county Clare, has a thirteenth-century friary, which in the Middle Ages had 350 friars and 600 students. The buildings were expanded over the years, and fully renovated in the 1950s.

THE BURREN

Northwest of Ennis, around 520sq km (200sq miles) of County Clare belongs to **the Burren** ㉗. Glaciers and ages of erosion have created limestone pavements – horizontal slabs divided by fissures, like the aftermath of an earthquake. Though sometimes described as a moonscape, the Burren is anything but barren; it is a quiet world of small animals, birds, butterflies, and alpine and Mediterranean flowers. It may seem hostile to human habitation, but the profusion of forts and tombs proves it supported a population for several centuries.

Geologists, botanists and archaeologists have field trips on the pavements, and speleologists enjoy the caves. More than 40km (25 miles) of caves have been fully explored. Most are for experts only, but anyone can visit **Aillwee Cave**, south-east of Ballyvaughan (www.aillweecave.ie). Kilfenora (www.kilfenoraclare.com) is famous for traditional Irish music, and the twelfth-century cathedral is noted for its sculptured monuments and high crosses. The **Burren Centre** (www.theburrencentre.ie) is a pleasant way to get your bearings.

The **Cliffs of Moher** ㉘, 10km (6 miles) northwest of Lahinch, tower 215m (700ft) over the Atlantic Ocean. From **O'Brien's Tower** (daily 9am–5pm Nov-Jan, Mar-Oct 8am-7pm, May-Aug 8am-9pm; www.cliffsofmoher.ie), an outpost near to the edge, the cliffs stand above the sea, revealing horizontal layers as easily defined as the storeys of a glass skyscraper. Huge waves crash against the foot of the cliff but the thump is heard late, like the report of a distant artillery shell. The cliffs are populated by thousands of seabirds.

The town of **Lisdoonvarna** was once famous as a spa. Today it is chiefly known for its Matchmaking Festival (www.matchmaker ireland.com) in September after the harvest, when farmers traditionally took a break from farming to seek a wife. The festival is a light-hearted affair, attracting some 40,000 hopeful visitors annually.

Across the border in County Galway, the area around Gort has a number of literary associations. Lady Gregory, co-founder of the Abbey Theatre, lived in **Coole Park**, now a nature reserve (all year; free) with Tea rooms (Wed, Thurs, Fri, Sat & Sun 10am–5pm; www.coolepark.ie). The unique 'autograph tree' is inscribed with the initials of some of her famous visitors – Augustus John, John Masefield, Sean O'Casey and one of the few who is instantly recognized by his initials: George Bernard Shaw.

GALWAY

The main city of the western province of Connaught, **Galway** ㉙ is a port, resort, administrative and cultural centre. In medieval times it prospered as a city-state, but withered in the seventeenth century after prolonged sieges by the forces of Oliver Cromwell and, four decades later, by William of Orange. Remnants of the old glory still shine in a few corners of the renewed city, with its vibrant young population.

The **Collegiate Church of St Nicholas** was begun by the Anglo-Normans in 1320 and is dedicated to the patron saint of seafarers, Saint Nicholas of Myra. According to local legend, Columbus came to pray here in 1477, long before his voyage to America. Today the area around the church is the venue for a lively Saturday morning food and craft market (http://galway market.com).

During Galway's heyday, 14 families – mostly of

A gargoyle on Lynch's Castle in Galway

Derryclare Lake in Connemara

Welsh and Norman descent – formed a sort of medieval Mafia that controlled the economic and political life of the town. Their common enemy, the O'Flaherty family, inspired the inscription (1549) over the old town gate: 'From the fury of the O'Flaherties, good Lord deliver us'.

Of the tribes in Galway, the Lynch family left the most memories and monuments. **Lynch's Castle**, a town house dating from 1600, is decorated with excellent stonework, gargoyles, and carved window frames. This unique building has been restored and now houses a bank.

Another reminder of the Lynches is the Lynch Memorial Window in Market St, with a plaque recounting the macabre story of James Lynch Fitzstephen – Mayor of Galway in 1493 – who condemned and executed his own son, Walter, for murder. Judge Lynch had to be the hangman because nobody else would agree to carry out the sentence.

Galway's Catholic cathedral – whose full name is the **Cathedral of Our Lady Assumed into Heaven and St Nicholas** – (daily 9am–6.30pm, www.galwaycathedral.ie) has a giant dome looming over the city. The classical architecture is misleading; the church was dedicated in 1965. Alongside the cathedral is Galway's **Salmon Weir**, in which salmon fight their way from the sea up to Lough Corrib. From June to July you can see them queueing up for a chance to leap up the falls and follow their instincts to sweet water.

Galway's seaside suburb, **Salthill**, is a traditional seaside resort with a long promenade and a clean sandy beach. It's a great place to watch the sun set on Galway Bay; sprawling hills enclose most of the bay, but the Atlantic can be seen to the west.

CONNEMARA

Lough Corrib, a loch extending 43km (27 miles) north from Galway, is big enough to be whipped by waves when the wind hurtles down the hillside. It's generally shallow and well supplied with islands and fish – salmon, trout, pike and perch. Lough Corrib divides County Galway into two contrasting regions: a fertile limestone plain to the east, and Connemara – a range of dramatic mountains and sparkling lakes – to the west, all enclosed by the coastline of rugged cliffs and pristine beaches.

Much of the south coast of Connemara is an Irish-speaking enclave. This is also the home of the Connemara pony – robust, intelligent and self-reliant. Spanish horses of the sixteenth century are rumoured to have crossbred with Irish ponies; one version says that the stallions swam ashore from ships when the Spanish Armada wrecked on nearby rocks.

The sky seems to change by the minute in the far west – dazzling sun, fleeting clouds and rain alternating so quickly that photographers have to be constantly at the ready. The capital is the well-placed market town of **Clifden** ③⓪, a base for exploring the nearby

Twelve Bens

The huge Twelve Bens of Connemara ('ben' is Gaelic for peak) constitute a range of moody mountains mostly inhabited by sheep; the foothills are interspersed with bogs and pretty lakes.

lakes and rivers, as well as fine beaches, bogs and mountains. The town's Irish name is *An Clochán*, meaning 'Stepping Stones'. There are so many areas of water around Clifden that you can't tell the genuine sea inlets from the coves of the lakes, except for the seaweed, a plant that features in Irish cooking more than you'd expect (usually called '*dulse*' or '*dillisk*'). Nearby is **Kylemore Abbey** (opening times vary); visitor centre free, gardens and abbey charge; www.kylemoreabbeytourism.ie), the home of Ireland's Benedictine nuns and one of the most photographed buildings in the country.

ARAN ISLANDS

Out in the Atlantic, 48km (30 miles) off Galway, the **Aran Islands** ③ (www.aranislands.ie) are a remote outpost indeed, little more than

Inishmore from above

stone outcrops. In the past islanders had to struggle to survive, cultivating the bleak limestone terrain, which had so little topsoil that they would ship it in from the mainland or scrape it from the cracks between the rocks and mix it with seaweed fertiliser to grow feed for their livestock. Tourism has now improved their fortunes, and though their famous Aran sweaters are still made here, these days few of them are hand-knitted. All the locals speak Gaelic in their daily life, but can also speak English.

Inishmore, 'the Big Island', is 14km- (9 miles-) from tip to tip and only 3km- (2 miles-) across. From the air – and you can fly there from Galway (www.aerarannislands.ie) – you can make out tapestries of tiny fields enclosed by dry-stone walls. **Kilronan** has a port where ferries from the mainland dock. The fishermen work aboard modern trawlers, but the traditional *currachs*, tar-coated boats with canvas hulls, are still used. This is an island to explore on foot or rented bicycle, available at the pier. If you're in a hurry, you can hire pony traps for guided tours, or the island even has a single motorised taxi which doubles as a school bus.

The remarkable monument of **Dún Aengus** (daily Mar 9.30am–4pm; end Mar–Oct 9.45am–7; Nov–Dec 9.30am–4pm; Jan–Feb Wed–Sun 9.30am–4pm), a giant prehistoric fortress on the sheer edge of a cliff some 91m (300ft) high, is about a 15-minute walk across the fields from the road. Three layers of stone walls, the outermost 6m (20ft) high, surround the courtyard 46m (150ft) across. With the ramparts and obstacles set up beyond the wall, the total area covers 4 hectares (11 acres). Even in modern times it would take a rash general to stage an attack on Dún Aengus.

Elsewhere on the islands, among colourful wild flowers, grazing cows, sheep and an abundance of bounding rabbits, there are numerous archaeological sites of minor importance that nevertheless have their own diversion to offer. Here you'll find stone

Croagh Patrick

forts and groups of primitive stone dwellings, as well as hermits' cells, round towers, holy wells, and ruined churches.

Inis Oírr (http://discover inisoirr.com) is the smallest island with a beautiful, sandy beach. An innovative arts centre, **Aras Eanna** (www.aras-eanna.ie/en), regularly hosts some of Ireland's top acts, including Tommy Tiernan and Damien Dempsey. Inis Oírr is instantly recognisable to fans of the TV classic 'Father Ted' as Craggy Island, look out for the Tedfest celebrations (http://tedfest.org) every February.

COUNTY MAYO

Rising high above Clew Bay, conical **Croagh Patrick** is Ireland's holy mountain. Every year thousands of pilgrims ascend the imposing summit, most of them on the last Sunday in July, and some barefoot. St Patrick is said to have spent Lent here in 441. There are views of the wide bay and the hills of counties Mayo, Clare and Galway.

Westport ㉜, at the head of Clew Bay, is an example of eighteenth-century urban planning. The Mall boulevard follows the Carrowbeg River. Outside the town, the home of the Marquess of Sligo can be visited. **Westport House** (daily, usually 10am–6pm but hours vary greatly so check online, closed Jan–Feb; www.westporthouse.ie) is palatial, with paintings, silver and glassware. There is a Pirate Adventure Park with flume rides and dungeons.

CRUISING THE RIVER SHANNON

The best place to hire a boat is Carrick-on-Shannon, the capital of County Leitrim and home to the superb Costello Chapel. Downstream, the river runs into Lough Corry, the first of many interconnected lakes in the Shannon basin. Lough Ree, halfway down, is 26km- (16 miles-) long and 11km- (7 miles-) wide, with deserted wooded islands.

The main cross-country roads ford the Shannon at the central market town of Athlone, with a medieval castle overlooking the Shannon Bridge. The town holds a number of festivals and cultural events. At a bend in the river is Clonmacnoise, an ancient monastic settlement founded in the sixth century by St Ciaran.

Just 6km (4 miles) south of Clonmacnoise, a 16-arch bridge marks Shannonbridge; at Shannon Harbour the Grand Canal from Dublin meets the river. Portumna is a fishing and boating resort with a new marina.

Lough Derg is the largest of the Shannon lakes – 40km- (25 miles-) long and up to 5km- (3 miles-) wide with islets and fair green hills beyond – a perfect end to the trip. This is just as well because dangerous rapids abound below Killaloe, a prudent place to abandon ship. Killaloe was once a great ecclesiastical centre, where St Flannan's Cathedral has been restored to its twelfth-century glory. The richly carved Romanesque doorway is said to be the entrance to the tomb of King Murtagh O'Brien of Munster (d. 1120). The granite shaft nearby, from about the year 1,000, bears a bilingual inscription in Runic and Ogham letters – a foretaste of today's Irish-English road signs.

Castlebar, a quiet partly Georgian town, is the county town of Mayo. To the east, in Turlough, **The National Museum of Country Life** ㉝ (Tue, Wed, Thurs, Fri & Sat 10am–5pm, Sun & Mon 1–5pm; free; www.museum.ie) houses the National Folklife Collection, a series of hugely entertaining displays illustrating rural life in Ireland from 1850 to about 1950.

Inland, the village of **Knock** (from the Irish *Cnoc Mhuire* – 'Mary's Hill') is a respected place of pilgrimage. In 1879 the townspeople saw an apparition of the Virgin Mary, St Joseph and St John on a south gable of the old parish church. In the centenary year of 1979, pilgrim Pope John Paul II came from Rome to address an open-air mass at Knock with over 400,000 of the faithful. Knock still caters to the pilgrims, with souvenir shops and a museum of folklore and handicrafts. The site of the famous apparition has been enclosed in glass, and statues recreate the position of the figures in the vision.

In **Foxford**, the old woollen mill houses an interpretative centre that tells the story of the famine in the area, while near Ballycastle, on the north Mayo cliffs, the pyramid-shaped heritage centre of **Céide Fields** (Mar–Sept daily 10am–6pm, Nov daily 10am–4.30; www.heritageireland.ie) uncovers the site of one of

SHAMROCK CURTAIN

Travelling in the west of Ireland you may cross the Shamrock Curtain, an important cultural frontier. Signs are printed in Gaelic letters and the people speak Irish as a first language. This is the Gaeltacht. Its residents strive to maintain Irish as a living language. The Dublin government actively supports Gaeltacht efforts to keep the old language and culture alive. Courses in Irish offered here every summer are a rite of passage for Irish teenagers.

the area's many prehistoric settlements. The site, dating back to 3000 BC, is estimated to be the single largest Stone Age monument in existence in the world today.

The country's biggest island, **Achill** , is buffeted by wind and tide, with meagre farms between ominous mountains and rocky shores. Despite this (or because of it) the scenery – from enormous cliffs to superb beaches – is truly

Sligo town

magnificent. Achill feels adrift, though you can drive there from the mainland across an unimpressive bridge. Driving on the island's deserted roads can revive the joy of motoring.

Prehistoric graves can be found on the harsh slopes of Achill's overpoweringly high mountain, the 672-m (2,204-ft) **Slievemore**. Driving offers the most vertigo-inducing cliff views and perspectives of the ocean churning round the off-islands and shoals. Inland, note the three-chimneyed cottages set between moors and bogs.

THE NORTHWEST

Sligo lies between two mountains, Ben Bulben and Knocknarea. The Vikings invaded here in 807. In 1252, Maurice Fitzgerald, the Earl of Kildare, founded **Sligo Abbey** (Apr–mid-Oct daily 10am– 6pm; www.heritageireland.ie), a Dominican friary. It burned down in 1414, but was soon rebuilt. It was attacked by Puritan troops in 1641, and the friars were killed. Its ruins combine desolation and grace. Three sides remain, and there are fine carvings.

The resort of **Strandhill**, west of Sligo, has a beach with long-rolling waves for surfers. **Knocknarea**, the flat-topped mountain over this stretch of shore, must have had a curious attraction for the early settlers, as the area abounds in megalithic monuments. A steep but manageable climb will bring you to the 328-m (1,078-ft) high summit of Knocknarea, where a large cairn is believed to mark the burial place of the first-century Queen Maeve of Connaught. This vantage point gives a fantastic, sweeping view across Sligo Bay. Awesome **Ben Bulben** looms in the distance, 526m- (1,730ft-) high. On its flat top you'll find arctic and alpine plants.

In the shadow of this majestic mountain is the small church of **Drumcliff**, with its turreted belfry. It was the desire of W.B. Yeats, who spent many childhood summer holidays around Sligo, to be laid to rest in the churchyard, 'Under bare Ben Bulben's head'.

About 27km (17 miles) to the north of Sligo, situated on the approach to the village of Mullaghmore, look out for the stunning **Classiebawn Castle**, which claims the skyline all to itself. This was the summer dwelling of Earl Mountbatten of Burma, who was assassinated by the IRA in 1979 when his fishing boat was blown up just off the shore nearby.

COUNTY DONEGAL

The most northerly county on the island, **Donegal** is known for its scenery – mountains, glens and lakes. This is also where Donegal homespun tweed comes from. **Donegal town** ㊱ has a medieval castle that occupies the site of a previous Viking fort. *Dun na nGall* in Irish means the 'Fortress of the Foreigners', a reference to the Vikings. On the edge of town, the ruins of Donegal Abbey overlook the estuary. West along the coast, **Killybegs** is a big fishing port; the trawlers here have wheelhouses with devices for tracking down the fish.

The road to the village of **Glencolumbkille** ❸ heads deep into spectacular country. Over the crest of a hill, you see the simple village below, enfolded in green hillsides that funnel down to the sea. In Irish the name *Glencolumbkille* means the 'Glen of St Colmcille' (or St Columba).

Today it is said that the sixth-century saint, who changed the course of history by introducing the Christian faith to Scotland, began his career by converting locals. The numerous old standing stones were formerly pagan monuments, which St Columba simply adapted to the new religion. On the saint's feast day, 9 June, pilgrims follow the pathway of these old stones. Over 40 prehistoric

Charming Donegal town

dolmens, souterrains and cairns have been catalogued in this area, some as old as 5,000 years.

Perched on a hilltop in Inishowen, you can visit the **Grianan Aileach Ring Fort** dating from 1700 BC. It is well-preserved and similar in style to Staigue Fort in Co Kerry. **Fort Dunree**, on the Inishowen peninsula overlooking Lough Swilly, is a fascinating military history museum in an old fort.

Glenveagh National Park ❸❽ (park daily dawn till dusk; visitor centre daily 9am–5pm; www.glenveaghnationalpark.ie) sprawls across 10,000 hectares (24,700 acres) of the most beautiful part of Co Donegal, with magnificent lakeside views from Glenveagh Castle. Nearby is **Glebe House and Gallery** (Jun–Oct Sat–Thu 11am–6.30pm; http://glebegallery.ie), an elegant Regency country house and gardens built in 1828. This was once the home of the artist Derek Hill, who bequeathed it along with his art collection to the Irish state in 1981.

NORTHERN IRELAND

Although a troubled region throughout much of the twentieth century, it's become hard to be sure of the exact location of the border between the Republic and Northern Ireland since the 1998 Good Friday Agreement led to a lessening of violence and the removal of army checkpoints. The border – a hot topic in the UK's Brexit negotiations – snakes its way along eighteenth-century county boundaries, through farming land that is sometimes bleak, more often breathtakingly beautiful, and takes little account of natural boundaries such as rivers, or of the cultural differences that separate Republican-minded Roman Catholics and Unionist-oriented Protestants. Houses straddle it so that, as the joke has it, a man may sleep with his head in the United Kingdom and his heart in the Republic of Ireland.

The Hands Across the Divide statue in Derry

Political expediency accounts for the absurdities. The intention was to redraw the border rationally after partition in 1920 left six of the nine counties of the ancient province of Ulster (Antrim, Down, Armagh, Derry, Fermanagh and Tyrone) under British rule, and a Boundary Commission was set up. But in the end the British and Irish governments, both hoping to avoid further trouble, suppressed the commission's report and left things as they were.

BELFAST

Belfast ㊲, the capital, looks little different from a provincial English city. **Donegall Place**, the 'main street', is lined with UK chain stores, while post boxes are no longer green, as in the Republic, but red. Sectarian tensions are, hopefully, a thing of the past: nowadays bus and taxi tours show visitors where the worst riots of the 1970s and 1980s took place.

Queen's University, Belfast

Set in a saucer of green hills and spanning the mouth of the River Lagan as it flows into the Irish Sea, Belfast is essentially a Victorian creation, its wealth founded on textile manufacturing and shipbuilding. Today most of the factories have vanished, though two towering yellow cranes (Samson and Goliath) survive as a reminder of the great days of Harland & Wolff shipyard, birthplace of the *Titanic*. In April 2011, the centenary of the *Titanic's* ill-fated voyage was marked by the opening of Titanic Belfast, the world's largest Titanic visitor experience.

Dominating the centre in Donegall Square is the 1906 **City Hall** Ⓐ the architecture of which has been dubbed 'Wrenaissance', in tribute to its shameless resemblance to Sir Christopher Wren's St Paul's Cathedral in London. Queen Victoria presides over the area outside, her statue supported by workers from the linen and shipbuilding industries. Inside, an ornate marble staircase sweeps up to the Rotunda, and the banqueting hall and council chamber are suitably extravagant. Among the marble statues around the City Hall is a **Titanic Memorial**, complete with weeping sea-nymphs.

To the north of the City Hall, Donegall Place, which becomes Royal Avenue, is Belfast's main shopping thoroughfare. **Linen Hall Library ❸**, on Donegall Square North, is a revered public-subscription library – a treasure house for historians and political journalists. Close by, on Great Victoria Street, are two architectural gems: the 1895 **Grand Opera House ❹** (www.goh.co.uk), with its plush brass and velvet, its gilded elephant heads and excellent acoustics, and the **Crown Liquor Saloon ❺**, a riot of Victorian Baroque, owned by the National Trust but still serving the finest Guinness and whisky.

Great Victoria Street leads on, via Shaftesbury Square, to the Tudor-style **Queen's University ❻**, whose central tower bears a suspicious resemblance to that of Magdalen College, Oxford. The university has colonised just about every available building in the vicinity, but welcome green space is provided by the adjacent **Royal Botanic Gardens ❼**, which contain a curvilinear Palm House. Beside the park is the revamped **Ulster Museum ❽** (Tue, Wed, Thurs, Fri, Sat & Sun 10am–5pm; free; http://nmni.com/um) which is noted for its well-presented displays of art, human history and natural sciences.

Belfast, of course, has many churches. Worth checking out are the neo-Romanesque **St Anne's Cathedral ❾** in Donegall Street, the extravagantly decorated interior of **St Malachy's Church ❿** in Clarence Street and the delightful **First Presbyterian Church ⓚ** in Rosemary Street.

Across the River Lagan, in the newly named Titanic Quarter, the **SSE Arena ⓚ** (www.ssearenabelfast.com) is a venue for sporting events and pop concerts, and hosts the children's science and discovery centre, **W5** (Mon, Tues, Wed, Thurs & Fri 10am–5pm, Sat 10am–6pm, Sun noon–6pm; www.w5online.co.uk). One of the

The Giant's Causeway

city's newer attractions, the **Titanic Belfast** ⓛ (seasonal opening hours; www.titanicbelfast.com) relives the ship's story in nine galleries, with full-scale reconstructions.

On the Newtownards Road, 10km (6 miles) from the centre, are the much-televised **Parliament Buildings** at Stormont, now the home of the Northern Ireland Assembly.

THE ANTRIM COAST ROAD

To the northeast of Belfast, past **Carrickfergus** (which has a fine Norman castle) and the industrial port of **Larne** ⓴, the lovely **Antrim Coast Road** runs alongside the Irish Sea through picturesque villages such as **Cushendall** and **Cushendun**. Diversions can be made along the way into any of the nine green glens, peaceful landscapes traditionally farmed.

The north coast begins at **Ballycastle** ㉑, setting for the Ould Lammas Fair (an agricultural fair held in August since 1606), and the ferry departure point for a 13km (8 mile) trip to **Rathlin Island**, whose population of 100 is vastly outnumbered by seabirds. Continuing east, you pass **Carrick-a-Rede Rope Bridge** (daily weather permitting; www.nationaltrust.org.uk/carrick-a-rede), which swings over a 24-m (80-ft) chasm, allowing salmon fishermen and brave tourists access to a rocky promontory (an activity so popular the National Trust has limited numbers and launched a pre-booking system: http://carrickaredetickets.com). Past cliffs and white surfers' beaches are the romantic ruins of the sixth-century **Dunseverick Castle**.

Bushmills is home to the world's oldest distillery (tours and whiskey tastings available; www.bushmills.com/distillery). It is also the jumping-off point for Ireland's most spectacular natural phenomenon, the **Giant's Causeway** 42 (coastline daily

MUSIC AND MURALS

Northern Ireland's popular culture portrays the sectarian divide with the bluntness of bombs and bullets. Triumphalist or threatening murals adorn the sides of hundreds of houses, particularly in Belfast and Derry. The Protestant versions often feature William of Orange, who defeated his Catholic father-in-law, James II, at the Battle of the Boyne in 1690. Catholic murals celebrate Republican heroes and aspirations. Balaclava-clad men brandishing rifles are common to both traditions. The worst murals are crudely executed; the best can be viewed as exceptional folk art.

For both Protestants and Catholics, marching bands keep history alive and mark out territory. The biggest parades are staged on 12 July by Protestant Orangemen (commemorating William of Orange). On the surface it's tuneful pageantry – but it can also be fiercely provocative.

dawn–dusk, visitor centre daily 9am–5pm, later in summer;
www.nationaltrust.org.uk/giants-causeway). Formed 60 million
years ago when molten lava froze into 38,000 basalt columns,
mostly hexagonal, it looks like a series of giant stepping-stones.
Park near the visitor centre or, in season, catch a narrow-gauge
steam locomotive from Bushmills. To the west are the resorts of
Portrush and **Portstewart**, and the ruins of the fourteenth-century **Dunluce Castle**.

DERRY CITY AND FERMANAGH

Protestants still call **Derry** , Northern Ireland's second city,
Londonderry, the name given to it by the London guilds who
began creating the walled city in 1614. The 6m- (20ft-) thick
walls boast watchtowers and cannons, such as the 1642 'Roaring
Meg'. The excellent **Tower
Museum**, in Union Hall
Place, relates the city's troubled history. **St Columb's
Cathedral**, in London Street,
is a graceful seventeenth-
century Anglican church.

3.5km (5 miles) north
of Omagh is The **Ulster
American Folk Park**
(Mar–Oct Tues, Wed, Thurs,
Fri, Sat & Sun 10am–5pm;
Nov–Feb Tues, Wed, Thurs
& Fri 10am–4pm, Sat & Sun
11am–4pm; http://nmni.
com/uafp). The rebuilt
craftsmen's cottages,
schoolhouse, and forge

The Guildhall Clocktower, Derry

recreate eighteenth-century living conditions here, while log cabins, and covered wagons illustrate the New World that many emigrants created in America. It is said that 11 US presidents had their roots in the province.

Further south, **Fermanagh** is the province's lakeland playground. Summer pleasure boats ply the lakes from the busy county town of **Enniskillen** ⓯. On Lower Lough Erne, **Boa Island** has an ancient two-faced Janus statue and **Devenish Island** has a fine round tower.

Heading back towards the east coast, **Armagh** ⓰ has two fine cathedrals (both called St Patrick's), some notable Georgian buildings and a planetarium. Just outside the town is **Navan Fort**, one of Ireland's most important historical sites – the ancient seat of the kings of Ulster.

MOUNTAINS OF MOURNE

Close to the Irish Sea, the 15 granite peaks of the **Mourne Mountains** ⓱ reach to more than 600m (2,000ft). At the summit of Slieve Donard are two cairns (ancient mounds of stones). From here, on a clear day, you can see Scotland, England, the Isle of Man, and Snowdonia in Wales.

Passing through **Downpatrick**, you can take the ferry from Strangford to Portaferry and drive up the **Ards Peninsula** ⓲, a 37km- (23 mile-) long finger dotted by villages and beaches. **Mount Stewart**, an eighteenth-century mansion, has one of Europe's greatest gardens.

At Cultra, near Holywood on the main road into Belfast, the **Ulster Folk Museum and Transport Museum** ⓳ (Mar–Sept Tue, Wed, Thurs, Fri, Sat & Sun 10am–5pm; Oct–Feb Tue, Wed, Thurs & Fri 10am–4pm, Sat and Sun 11am–4pm; http://nmni.com/uftm) are set in 70 hectares (170 acres) of a green and picnic-friendly woodland park.

Walking in the Mourne Mountains

THINGS TO DO

SPORTS

Whether on land or sea (or river or lake), the Irish enjoy so many sporting activities that we can only touch on a handful of the most popular. If you are interested in more specialist sports, such as kite-surfing, hang-gliding, or even polo, the tourist board (see page 129) can put you in touch with the appropriate sports associations.

Golf. In a country so green, you might scarcely notice the vast number of golf courses, but there are more than 400, including several of championship status. Some clubs are private, but not rigorously so: while you might find that non-members are excluded over the weekend, you'll have few problems on weekdays. See www.golf.discoverireland.ie for more details.

Greyhound racing. This is a very popular pursuit. Teams of hare-brained dogs keep eager gamblers busy six nights a week in Dublin – which has two greyhound stadiums – and elsewhere in Ireland. See www.grireland.ie.

Horse racing. Almost everyone in Ireland seems to be totally engrossed, one way or another, in the sport of kings. Dublin boasts several famous courses within easy reach. The flat season is from March to November, and steeplechasing goes on all year. See www.goracing.ie for information on events.

Horse riding. Stables can be found all over Ireland with fine Irish horses, beautiful ponies, and trekking routes through delightful verdant countryside.

National games. Hurling, which has been played for 4,000 years, is a very fast and exciting high-scoring game where a small, leather ball (*sliotar*) is struck with a wooden hurley (like hockey but at head height). Gaelic football, Ireland's other traditional sport, ostensibly resembles a marriage between soccer and rugby and can often be quite rough and ready too with passionate players and a fast pace on the ground. For more information on Gaelic sporting events and the history of the sports, visit www.gaa.ie.

Imported games. Rugby union (www.irishrugby.ie) and soccer (www.fai.ie) are very popular, while hockey (www.hockey.ie), basketball (www.basketballireland.ie) and cricket (www.cricketireland. ie) also have a following.

Walking and cycling. Both have grown in popularity, with some 32 long-distance walking routes, and dedicated cycle routes, such as the Great Western Greenway (www.greenway.ie) in Co Mayo. See www.discoverireland.ie/walking-and-hiking or www.discover ireland.ie/cycling.

WATERSPORTS

Sailing. Watersports of all kinds are popular in Ireland, with its long, indented coastline. Hire a yacht with or without a skipper, or get afloat in a simple kayak. See www.discoverireland.ie, https:// canoe.ie and www.sailing.ie.

Scuba diving. Popular all over Ireland – mostly in the summer months, as the water can get mighty cold. Along the north coast there are lots of wreck dives, with Spanish galleons from the Armada resting beneath the waves. For a list of dive centres see www.scuba.ie.

Sea fishing. From a long sandy beach, a pier, a clifftop or a boat, you can hook big beautiful trophies of the deep, such as shark, sea bass, tope, skate, halibut, conger and many more. Details at www. discoverireland.ie/angling.

Swimming. Blue Flag beaches have to meet certain safety criteria, including having adequate life-saving equipment and, if necessary, lifeguards on duty and beautiful beaches can be found all along the country's coastline. For a list of Blue Flag beaches all over Ireland, visit www.blueflagireland.org.

Surfing. The heavy Atlantic swells are more impressive on the west coast, where the biggest surfing bases are Lahinch Co Clare, Strandhill Co Sligo, Bundoran Co Donegal, and Tramore Co Waterford, on the east coast. See www.surfaroundireland.com.

Boating. Cruising the inland waterways in a rented cabin cruiser makes a great break, especially on the River Shannon. You can also try more energetic sports such as canoeing or paddleboarding. See www.discoverireland.ie, www.leitrimsurf.ie and www.waterwaysireland.org.

Game fishing. Fertile salmon fisheries are mostly restricted, but arrangements can be made – though preferably well in advance.

Riding ponies on Cleggan Beach in Connemara

Trout are abundant in rivers and lakes; as with salmon, you will need a licence. Details at www.discoverireland.ie/angling.

SHOPPING

Friendly sales staff make shopping in Ireland a real pleasure. The most appealing products are made by Irish craftsmen in traditional or new styles; the Kilkenny Design Centre in Kilkenny City has a particularly fine range of traditional goods on offer. The Design and Crafts Council's website at www.dcci.ie is also a good starting point that enables you to research what's available in the area you're visiting.

For clothes or slightly more eclectic souvenirs, Dublin is the place to visit. It offers shoppers everything from upscale boutiques to huge shopping malls: check out the vast **Dundrum Town Centre** (www.dundrum.ie), just outside Dublin city centre, or the more intimate **Powerscourt Centre** (www.powerscourtcentre.ie). **Grafton Street** is the main shopping street, with high street names and fashionable department stores such as the much-loved Brown Thomas (www.brownthomas.com). Other interesting shops include the **House of Names** (www.houseofnames.ie), Nassau Street, whose handmade

Traditional bodhráns

coats of arms allegedly feature the crests of more than 96 percent of the world's surnames; and **George's Street Arcade** (www.georgesstreetarcade.ie), just off South Great George's, a vibrant indoor market with an eclectic worldwide mix of goods, from Greek olives to Peruvian handwoven rugs.

WHAT TO BUY

Aran jumpers. Demand so far exceeds supply that they are now made in mainland factories as well as on the Aran islands. For genuinely hand-knitted jumpers, go to Blarney Woollen Mills (www.blarney.com) in Cork, Ó'Máille (www.omaille.com) in Galway and Cleo Ltd (www.cleo-ltd.com) in Dublin.

Connemara marble. A rich green, this stone is unique to Ireland. All sorts of souvenirs are made from Connemara marble, especially jewellery.

Chocolate. Buy delicious hand-made chocolates at Butler's Irish Chocolates in Grafton Street, Dublin, and at the Skelligs Chocolate Factory in Ballinskelligs, Co Kerry. Try before you buy at the Lir Cafés in Killarney, Co Kerry and Carrigaline, Co Cork.

Metal working. Enamel bowls, plaques, and pendants by master craftspeople.

Crosses. Reproductions of old Christian crosses and St Brigid crosses made out of straw.

Toys. In Dublin, Avoca (www.avoca.com) and Arnotts (www.arnotts.ie) both have extensive toy departments. Current favourites are Bumblebee Creations (www.bumblebeecreations.ie – check out their kids' hurling kit, the 'Hurlóg') and craft creations from Little Green Dot (www.littlegreendot.ie).

Glassware. Waterford crystal, world renowned, is still available even though the factory has closed. Jerpoint Glass in County Kilkenny produces hand-blown uncut crystal in contemporary designs.

Jewellery. Celtic designs inspire many of today's goldsmiths and silversmiths, while others work in a contemporary style. In Dublin, head to DesignYard (www.designyard.ie) for high-end Irish jewellery.

Lace. Although a waning trade in Limerick and Co Monaghan, there is now a strong revival of lacemaking in Carrickmacross, Clones, Kenmare, and Youghal.

Linen. Weaving continues in Northern Ireland, with a huge emphasis on quality. Irish Linen should bear the Irish Linen Guild's trademark, see www.irishlinen.co.uk. Brands such as Thomas Ferguson and Baird McNutt are heirloom quality.

Paintings. Artists produce fine studies of Ireland, including landscapes, seascapes, flora and fauna, in oils, watercolours, prints, and etchings. Check out Merrion Square (www.merrionart.com) in Dublin on the weekend year round to source unique pieces of art.

Peat. Even the turf of Ireland is compressed and sculpted to reproduce ancient religious and folklore symbols.

Pottery. Traditional and modern designs, sought after by collectors. Kiltrea Bridge Pottery from Co Wexford and Nicholas Mosse Pottery from Co Kilkenny are always in fashion.

Rushwork. In a land rich in thatched cottages, the makers of woven baskets and similar wickerwork still thrive.

Smoked salmon. Fish specially packed for travelling is on sale at the airport. Opt for wild salmon that is certified organic.

Souvenirs. Leprechauns, marble worry stones, and *shillelaghs* (short wooden clubs) are all widely available. Books about Irish history make easy-to-carry souvenirs. GAA jerseys are a quirky gift – wear your county colours with pride!

Tweed and Wool. Handwoven fabrics in a variety of colours and weights, traditionally weaved in Donegal. Check out Magee (www.magee1866.com) on Wicklow St, Dublin and McNutt of Donegal in the Gaeltacht village of Downings, Co Donegal.

Wood turning. Many wood turners use only storm-damaged timber, making an ecologically sound product.

ENTERTAINMENT

TRADITIONAL MUSIC

Many hotels and pubs provide entertainment, featuring a diverse cross-section of traditional Irish entertainment: folk singers, harpists, dancers, and storytellers. In local pubs 'trad' (traditional) sessions can break out at any moment, with singers and musicians joining in. At the other end of the scale, luxury hotels put on elaborate productions. The shows have a typically Irish mixture of hand-clapping high spirits and 'Come Back to Erin' nostalgia. Jigs and reels are tirelessly

Trad music session in a local pub

danced, and lively tap dancers revive some of the country's oldest and best routines. *Bodhrans* (Irish drums), banjos, bagpipes, and accordions are all played with gusto, and fast fiddlers are ubiquitous.

You will find more genuine versions of traditional Irish music at *fleadhanna*, festivals of music and song around the island, climaxing in the All Ireland *Fleadh* in August. Tourist offices will have detailed schedules of such events (www.fleadhnua.com).

CLUBS AND BARS

The traditional pub is the heartbeat of Irish life and you can still find the real thing all over the country. Find traditional drinking holes like Dublin's ancient Brazen Head on Bridge Street Lower and, in Belfast, the Crown Liquor Saloon on Great Victoria Street (see page 83). Both will be full of tourists, but are worth it.

Dublin has a lively clubbing scene, centring on the **Temple Bar** and **Harcourt Street** areas. The better clubs have world-class DJs and regular live acts. The Button Factory (www.buttonfactory. ie) features a range of live music, and late-night themed events. Older sophisticates will enjoy the atmosphere at The Sugar Club on Leeson Street (www.thesugarclub.com).

MEDIEVAL MAYHEM

Restored medieval castles host grandiose candlelit banquets with traditional stories, poems, and songs. If you prefer not to drive, some package tours offer door-to-door transportation. Popular venues include Bunratty and Knappogue Castles in Co Clare and Dunguaire Castle in Co Galway (www.dunguairecastle.com).

THEATRE

Ireland's grand theatrical tradition – which gave the world Goldsmith, Shaw, Sheridan, Beckett, O'Casey, and more recently Conor McPherson and Martin McDonagh – continues in major towns such as Dublin, Belfast, and Cork. Tickets are usually available on the night at Ireland's National Theatre, the Abbey Theatre (www.abbeytheatre.ie) and the Gate Theatre (www.gatetheatre.ie) in Dublin. See www.entertainment.ie for full listings of concerts, theatre, and film.

CHILDREN

Fun outings for children of all ages include:
Bray promenade, 19km (12 miles) south of Dublin. Seaside resort with dodgems, amusement arcades, and an aquarium. **Bunratty Castle and Folk Park**, Co Clare, tel: (061) 360 788, www.bunrattycastle.ie. Costumed guides recreate life in olden times. Open daily year-round.

County Clare's beaches are popular with families

Clara-Lara, Vale of Clara, Co Wicklow, tel: (0404) 46161, www.clara lara.ie. Fun park, trout farm, and amusements. Summer only.

Imaginosity, Sandyford, Co Dublin, tel: (01) 217 6130, www.imagin osity.ie. A fun, educational space for children.

Dublin Zoo, tel: (01) 474 8900, www.dublinzoo.ie. A wide variety of animals and educational programmes.

Exploris, Portaferry, Co Down, tel: (028) 4272 8062, www.exploris. com. Discover creatures of the deep.

Farm visits. Many farms open to visitors and are ideal for kids. Tourist information offices (see page 129) have details.

National Aquatic Centre, Dublin, tel: (01) 646 4300, www.aqua zone.ie. Ireland's biggest swimming pool and best water rides.

Fota Wildlife Park, Carrigtwohill, Co Cork, tel: (021) 481 2678, www.fotawildlife.ie. This large park opens year-round.

National Gallery of Ireland, Dublin, tel: (01) 661 5133, www. nationalgallery.ie. Frequent children's activities.

National Wax Museum, Dublin, tel: (01) 671 8373, www.wax museumplus.ie. Historical and celebrity wax figures and chamber of horrors.

Newbridge Demesne, Co Dublin, tel: (01) 843 6534, www.new bridgehouseandfarm.com. Eighteenth-century house with farm and animals.

The Steam Museum, Co Kildare, tel: (01) 628 8412, www.steam-museum.ie, has model and full-sized steam engines; May–Sept.

Kerry County Museum, tel: (066) 712 7777, www.kerrymuseum.ie, in Tralee has a child-friendly Medieval Experience.

 Wells House & Gardens, Co Wexford, tel: (053) 918 6737, www. wellshouse.ie. Gruffalo and dragon enchanted woodland walking trails, playground and animal farm.

Viking Splash Tours, Dublin, tel: (01) 707 6000, www.vikingsplash. ie. Put on a Viking helmet and explore land and sea in a vintage World War II amphibious vehicle.

WHAT'S ON

January: *TradFest Temple Bar*, Dublin – traditional and folk music festival; *Shannonside Winter Music Weekend*, Co Clare – acoustic music festival.

February: *Dublin International Film Festival*.

March: *St Patrick's Week* – celebrations throughout Ireland; Killarney Mountain Festival – outdoor sport and adventure; *Dine in Dublin* – food festival.

April: *Pan-Celtic International Festival* – music, song, dance, and cultural events; *Irish Grand National Weekend at Fairyhouse*, Co Meath; *The Cork International Choral Festival*; *West Waterford Festival of Food*.

May: *Irish Open Golf Championships*; *Fleadh Nua* – traditional music and dance in Ennis, Co Clare; *Listowel Writers Week*, Co Kerry; *Slieve Bloom Walking Festival*, Kinnitty, Co Offaly; *Cat Laughs Comedy Festival*, Kilkenny.

June: Bloomsday, celebration of James Joyce on the day his novel Ulysses is set, Dublin; *Great Music in Irish Houses Chamber Music Festival*, all over Ireland; *Cork Midsummer Festival* – huge arts festival; SeaFest, Cork; *Irish Derby*, Curragh racecourse, Co Kildare.

July: *Galway Races*; *Galway Arts Festival*; *Lady of the Lake Festival*, Enniskillen, Co Fermanagh; *Earagail Arts Festival* – music and arts festival, Co Donegal.

August: *Connemara Pony Show*, Clifden, Co Galway; *Kilkenny Arts Festival*; *Oul' Lammas Fair*, Ballycastle, Co Antrim; *Puck Fair* – parades and family fun in Killorglin, Co Kerry; *Stradbally National Steam Rally*, Co Laois; *Rose of Tralee International Festival, Kerry*

September: *GAA All-Ireland Senior Hurling Final*, Dublin; *Clarenbridge Oyster Festival*, Galway; *Dublin Theatre Festival*; *Lisdoonvarna Matchmaking Festival*, Co Clare – traditional matchmaking amid much merriment.

October: *Kinsale Gourmet Festival*, Co Cork; *Bram Stoker Festival*, Dublin; *Ballinasloe Fair*, Co Galway – Europe's oldest horse fair; *Cork Jazz Festival*; Wexford Opera Festival; *Belfast Festival at Queen's*, huge arts festival.

November: *National Circus Festival Ireland*, Tralee, Co Kerry – watch and learn circus skills; *Dublin Beatles Festival* – celebration of the fab four.

December: *Glow – a Cork Christmas Celebration*; *Leopardstown Christmas Festival*; *Limerick Christmas Racing Festival*; *Guinness Choir Christmas Concert*, St Patrick's Cathedral, Dublin, Wonderlights (venue changes annually).

FOOD AND DRINK

Pubs are popular lunch or dinner spots, and they range from traditional taverns serving up sandwiches and salads to cosmopolitan gastro pubs. Cafés provide relaxed brunches and afternoon teas and there are luxurious restaurants offering Michelin-starred cuisine. Vegetarians are pretty well catered for these days, and the trend for locally-sourced artisan food has greatly enhanced the choice at all price levels.

Dublin's days of overcooked cabbage and cholesterol-laden fried meat are long gone. The city is increasingly sophisticated in its array and quantity of restaurants, and is matching other European capitals as a hotbed for talented and innovative chefs.

The English Market, Cork city

It can be expensive, though.

Kinsale, a small town in Co Cork, and Kenmare, a village in Co Kerry have both been called the 'gourmet capital' of Ireland. Cork and Galway have a good choice of casual city centre restaurants, while Belfast takes its culinary reputation seriously, and has a wide choice of adventurous eateries. Outside Dublin and Belfast ethnic restaurants in Ireland tend to be expensive and run-of-the-mill.

Alfresco dining

You don't have to look far to find an idyllic setting for a picnic in Ireland. Farmhouse cheeses, smoked salmon, freshly baked bread, and seasonal produce supply the ingredients. As for the setting, chose from the dramatic winding coastline, romantic forest parks or moody mountain views. The only thing that can't be guaranteed is the weather.

Ireland's Blue Book of Country Houses is a good source for exploring Ireland's famous castle hotels and stately homes. Don't miss the chance to enjoy a meal at one of Dublin's top restaurants. Lunch is often half the price of dinner and may include specials.

If you're on a budget, many small cafes and tearooms are good value. Look out for pubs offering 'carvery lunches' – a self-service option with generous portions of the roast of the day, a choice of potatoes, and assorted vegetables for around €10.

There is also the ever-present 'chippy' (fish and chip shop). Often the traditional end to a night in the pub, they also make a cheap, tasty and quick option to eating out. Thanks to the long coastline, the fish is always fresh and often cooked to order.

In addition to VAT (value added tax, which ranges from 9–23 percent in the Republic and is fixed at 20 percent in Northern Ireland), some upmarket restaurants add a service charge to the bill; extra tips are given at about 10 percent of the total bill.

WHEN TO EAT

Breakfast is served from about 7–10am, though in some hotels, matching the general leisurely air, it does not begin until 8am. Lunchtime is from 12.30–2.30pm, give or take half an hour at either end. The time of the evening meal depends on where you are. In rural areas and perhaps the less sophisticated town areas, people dine as early as 6pm. In the major towns and cities, however, you can eat any time from 6–10pm.

WHAT TO EAT

Breakfast

A real Irish breakfast starts the day superbly. You'll feel ready for any kind of exertion after a menu of juice, porridge, or cold cereal with milk or cream, fried eggs with bacon and sausages, toast or tasty homemade soda bread, butter, marmalade, tea or coffee. The quality of the bacon and sausages has improved enormously with the surge in artisan butchers.

In Ulster an important constituent of the breakfast fry-up is fried *farl* (potato bread). Irish soda bread, white or brown, is made from flour and buttermilk, bicarbonate of soda and salt; it's as delicious as cake. Black pudding, a heavy sausage filled with grains and blood, is a treat you'll either love or hate.

Other Meals

Irish soups are usually thick and hearty: vegetables, barley and meat stock with a dab of cream, for instance. Look for potato soup made out of potatoes, onions, carrots and parsley.

Fish caught fresh from the Atlantic, the Irish Sea or the island's streams is incredibly good. Keep an eye out for some of these great Irish delights: fresh salmon (poached or grilled), smoked salmon, sole and trout from the sea and rivers. Dublin Bay prawns are a big natural resource worthy of their fame, as are Galway oysters (often accompanied by a bottle of stout). With luck you could be offered mussels or lobster, but the great bulk of the catch is usually exported to the Continent.

Meat of the highest quality is at the heart of Irish cuisine. As is common in restaurants around the world, it is generally served simply to allow the fine flavour to speak for itself. The beef is excellent, but there is very little veal. You'll have a choice of roast beef or sumptuous steaks (T-bone, filet mignon or sirloin) served with elegant sauces, seasonal vegetables and buttery potatoes. Lamb appears as tender chops or as a roast, when not the main ingredient in Irish stew, a filling casserole of meat, potatoes, carrots and onions, laced with parsley and thyme. Irish pork products – bacon, sausages, chops and Limerick ham – are also rightly famous.

Galway Bay oysters

Dublin coddle is a delicious stew of sausages, bacon, onions, potatoes and parsley, a favourite for Saturday night supper in the capital. Venison is another popular choice at quality restaurants, as is rabbit or hare.

Potatoes have been a mainstay of the Irish diet since the seventeenth century, and a choice of roast, mashed or chips with your main course is not unusual. Mushrooms, which thrive in the cool, humid atmosphere here, are the single biggest horticultural export.

More and more restaurants are now serving vegetarian and vegan dishes, and fresh produce from Ireland's farms is a dream come true for those thinking Irish food is nothing more than meat and dairy.

Desserts are usually served with lashings of thick cream or ice cream – expect cheesecakes, homemade cakes and tarts, apple pies, and crumbles.

WHAT TO DRINK

A jug of tap water is often found on the table, and for many diners it's the only drink during the meal. Ireland has many brands of bottled spring water, widely sold and served in pubs and restaurants, and water is gaining popularity as a substitute for alcoholic drinks, especially at lunchtime. Some restaurants have a full licence to serve any drinks; otherwise, they serve wine only and not beer.

Irish pubs are usually as relaxed and friendly as their regular clients. Most are open all day, and most also serve tea and freshly made coffee. In rural areas the pub may not open until 6pm or later. Closing time is normally around midnight; sometimes later on Friday and Saturday nights. Pubs serving food or providing entertainment can apply for a licence to open later still. Some pubs in Northern Ireland may be shut on Sundays.

The Irish drink nearly 500 million pints of beer a year, mostly stout – a rich, creamy, dark brown version. Cork's two brands of

Traditional Irish pub

stout, Beamish and Murphy's, have become increasingly popular. In many a pub the simple order 'a pint, please' means 568ml of Guinness, lovingly drawn from the keg, scraped and topped. The pouring and settling process takes a little time, but it's worth the wait. The head is so thick that the barman can leave the image of a shamrock sitting within it. A 'glass' of stout means half a pint.

Irish lagers, craft ales and IPAs are becoming increasingly popular, and are also worth exploring. An interesting Irish drink, 'Black Velvet', combines stout and champagne, and is said to be good for hangovers.

The word whiskey (note the different spelling to Scottish 'whisky') comes from the Gaelic *uisce beatha*, 'water of life'. Irish whiskey is triple distilled (once more than Scotch), is matured in wooden casks for at least seven years and drunk neat, or with a little water – never with ice. You'll see the names of Irish whiskeys etched in the glass of pub windows.

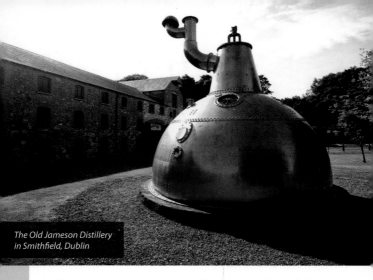

The Old Jameson Distillery in Smithfield, Dublin

Enthusiasts can visit the world's oldest whiskey distillery, Bushmills (www.bushmills.com), in Northern Ireland; it has held a licence since 1609. There's also the Old Jameson Distillery in Smithfield, the heart of old Dublin, and the Old Midleton Distillery just outside Cork; both are owned by Jameson. For further information go to www.jamesonwhiskey.com.

Whiskey features in many of Ireland's unusual and delicious drinks: Irish coffee, in a stemmed glass, is hot coffee laced with whiskey and sugar, with a tablespoonful of thick cream floating on top.

Two Irish liqueurs merit a try: Irish mist, the combination of honey, herbs and whiskey tingle on the palate; and Irish cream liqueur. Baileys launched Irish cream liqueur in the 1970s. Since then, Carolan's, Sheridan's and St Brendan's have all given it their own unique spin. Made with whiskey, chocolate and cream – like a leprechaun's milkshake, they say – it is very popular with coffee.

WHERE TO EAT

To give you an idea of prices, we have used the following symbols for a three-course meal for one excluding wine:

€€€	over €40	£££	over £35
€€	€20–40	££	£15–35
€	under €20	£	under £15

DUBLIN

Chapter One Restaurant €€–€€€ *18/19 Parnell Square, Dublin 1, tel: (01) 873 2266,* www.chapteronerestaurant.com. Thurs, Fri & Sat 12.30–2pm, Tues, Wed, Thurs, Fri & Saturday 6.30–9.30pm. This establishment, in the basement of the Dublin Writers Museum, is one of the city's best. The menu is classically French and takes its cheese and wine very seriously. Located just across from the Gate Theatre. Reservations advised.

Cornucopia € *19/20 Wicklow Street, Dublin 2, tel: (01) 677 7583,* www. cornucopia.ie. Mon & Tues 9am–8pm, Wed, Thurs, Fri & Sat 9am–9pm, Sun 10.30am–8pm. A vegetarian and vegan restaurant offering simple, delicious meals such as Turkish bean casserole, tasty salads and wholemeal breads. Great place for breakfast too. Self-service.

Elephant and Castle €–€€ *18 Temple Bar, Dublin 2, tel: (01) 533 7563,* www. elephantandcastle.ie. Daily 12–10pm. This is one of the most popular informal restaurants in the city. Quality burgers, salads and brunch options that bring a little bit of New York to Dublin. Vegetarian options. Also in Monkstown (18a Monsktown Crescent, tel: 01-572 0630) and Rathmines (272 Rathmines Road Lower, tel: 01-572 0600).

Ely Winebar €€ *22 Ely Place, St Stephen's Green, Dublin 2, tel (01) 676 8986,* www.elywinebar.ie. Wed, Thurs, Fri & Sat 3pm–8:30pm. Experience the elegance of old Dublin in this classic wine-bar restaurant near the Shelbourne Hotel. Over 70 wines served by the glass, and delicious organic food from the family farm. Also in Kildare (Convent Lane, Maynooth, tel: 01-504 3709).

Fallon & Byrne – Dining Room Restaurant €–€€ *11/17 Exchequer Street, Dublin 2, tel: (01) 472 1010, www.fallonandbyrne.com.* Daily 12–3pm, Sun, Mon & Tues 5.30–9pm, Fri & Sat 5.30–11pm. The classic French brasserie, The Dining Room, occupies the spacious second floor of the former telephone exchange. On the ground floor there is a take-away deli, descend to the atmospheric Cellar Bar for boutique wines and tapas.

The Vintage Kitchen €€ *7 Poolbeg Street, Dublin 2, tel: (01) 679 8705, www. thevintagekitchen.ie.* Daily, noon–10pm. Cosy eatery specialising in Irish food and local ingredients. Mouth-watering menus frequently change. Some vintage arts and crafts for sale. It's better to book in advance because the restaurant is rather small.

CORK

Ballymaloe House €€€ *Shanagarry, tel: (021) 465 2531, www.ballymaloe.ie.* Tues–Sat 6.30–9pm. This Georgian country house set on 160 hectares (400 acres) also houses a hotel, a cookery school, a craft and specialist kitchenware shop. Run by the Allen family, much noted for their gourmet cooking. Meals are served in the house's cosy dining rooms. Produce is grown in the gardens. The cuisine fits the setting and perfects the tradition of Irish country food.

Jacobs on the Mall €€€ *30a South Mall, Cork, tel: (021) 425 1530, www.jacobs onthemall.com.* Tues, Wed, Thurs, Fri & Sat 5–10pm. Local free-range and organic produce are used to create modern European dishes at this airy, contemporary restaurant in Cork City's financial district. There's also a piano bar and private dining room.

Mary Ann's Bar and Restaurant €€ *Castletownshend, County Cork, tel: (028) 36146.* Daily noon–9pm. Seafood restaurant with cheaper menus served from the bar; the restaurant is set in a small, idyllic seaside village in West Cork. The bar dates back to 1846.

GALWAY

Ard Bia at Nimmo's €–€€ *Spanish Arch, Galway City, tel: (091) 561 114, www. ardbia.com.* Café daily 10am–3pm; restaurant daily 6–9pm. A stone warehouse building on Galway's quayside has a cheerful café with fresh organic food downstairs and a flamboyantly decorated restaurant upstairs serving more formal fare. Great food in a great atmosphere.

The Kings Head Bistro €€ *Old Malt Arcade, 15 High Street, Galway City, tel: (091) 567 866, www.thekingshead.ie.* Mon, Tues, Wed, Thurs, Fri & Sat 12.30–10pm. A gastro-pub set in a charming courtyard adjoining the centuries' old King's Head pub. The décor is rustic and the menu focuses on local seafood and steaks, with killer cocktails.

McDonagh's Fish & Chip Bar € *22 Quay Street, Galway City, tel: (091) 565 001, www.mcdonaghs.net.* Mon, Tues, Wed, Thurs, Fri & Sat 12–10pm, Sun 1–9pm. Enjoy, freshly cooked, traditional fish and chips at this long-established Galway institution.

Gaslight Bar and Brasserie €€–€€€ *Hotel Meyrick, Eyre Square, Galway, tel: (091) 564 041, www.hotelmeyrick.ie.* Daily 7am–10pm. Newly refurbished restaurant overlooking Eyre Square; serves up first-class cuisine in bright, airy surroundings. Great place for drinks with an extensive wine list and cocktail menu. A hub for Galway's social scene.

KERRY

Bricin Restaurant €€ *26 High Street, Killarney, tel: (064) 663 4902, www.bricin. ie.* Tue, Wed, Thurs, Fri & Sat 6–9.30pm. Family run restaurant serving quality, traditional Irish food. Bricin is Gaelic for small trout and is also the name of a well-known bridge in Killarney National Park. There is a craft shop for a shot of Irish design.

The Chart House €€ *The Mall, Dingle, tel: (066) 915 2255, www.thecharthouse dingle.com.* Daily 5.30–11pm. This informal, award-winning cottage restaurant has a warm welcome. The high standard of cuisine concentrates on freshly-caught fish and local artisan food.

Lime Tree Restaurant €€ *Shelbourne Street, Kenmare, tel: (064) 664 1225, www.limetreerestaurant.com.* Thu, Fri, Sat, Sun & Mon 6–9.30pm. This converted former schoolhouse is home to a serious restaurant serving mainstream and modern Irish cuisine. Wide-ranging menu to suit all tastes and interesting wine list.

Park Hotel €€€ *Kenmare, tel: (064) 664 1200,* www.parkkenmare.com. The Outdoor Terrace, daily 6.30am–9pm, The Dining Room restaurant, daily 6.30–9pm. One of Ireland's finest country house hotels, the Park's restaurant uses the finest local produce and offers an a la carte menu daily. Take afternoon tea on the terrace, and enjoy stunning views of the gardens and Kenmare Bay.

KILKENNY

Campagne €€ *Kilkenny, tel: (053) 777 2858,* www.campagne.ie. Wed & Thu 5.30–9pm, Fri–Sat 5–9.30pm, Sun 6–8pm (bank holidays only). Upmarket French restaurant focusing on regional French cuisine made with seasonal ingredients – expect beef braised in wine and wild venison in winter alongside roasted fish and vegetarian-friendly plates such as smoked aubergine and ricotta gnudi. Naturally, great French desserts, wine and cheese too.

LIMERICK AND SHANNON

Cullinan's Seafood Restaurant €€ *Doolin, County Clare, tel: (065) 707 4183,* www.cullinansdoolin.com. Mon, Tues, Thurs, Fri & Sat 6–9pm. A simple, cottage restaurant, Cullinan's serves fresh local produce, including Burren smoked salmon, Doolin crabmeat, Aran Island scallops, locally-raised lamb and beef, and Irish farmhouse cheeses.

Earl of Thomond Restaurant Dromoland Castle €€€ *Newmarket-on-Fergus, County Clare, tel: (061) 368 144,* www.dromoland.ie/dining. Daily 7–9.30pm. The dining room in Dromoland Castle is spectacular, with superb, table settings and grand chandeliers overhead. Smart dress is essential at this 5-star hotel.

The Locke Bar and Restaurant €–€€ *George's Quay, Limerick, tel: (061) 413 733,* www.lockebar.com. Mon, Tues, Wed, Thurs & Fri 9am–11.30pm, Sat & Sun 10am–11.30pm. Award-winning gastro-pub. Famous for its seafood, fresh daily specials, and traditional Irish music sessions.

The Mustard Seed at Echo Lodge €€€ *Newcastle West Road, Ballingarry, tel: (069) 68508,* www.mustardseed.ie. Daily 6.30–9.30pm. Elegant four-course dining in a small Victorian country house hotel. Come for great food and a warm unstuffy ambiance. Smart casual dress.

Sash Restaurant at No. 1 Pery Square €€–€€€€ *Pery Square, Limerick, tel: (061) 402 402,* www.oneperysquare.com. Breakfast daily, lunch Tues, Wed, Thurs, Fri, Sat & Sun, dinner Tues, Wed, Thurs, Fri & Sat. On the first floor of this Georgian townhouse is Sash, so called in reference to the building's original Georgian sash windows. This restaurant is stylish yet cosy with a focus on fresh, locally sourced, seasonal ingredients. Wine and artisan food shop on site for goodies to go.

WATERFORD

Cliff House Hotel €€€ *Ardmore, Co Waterford, tel: (024) 87800,* www.the cliffhousehotel.com. Restaurant Tues, Wed, Thurs, Fri & Sat from 6.30pm, advance booking recommended. Luxury boutique hotel with sensational clifftop location and award-winning, Michelin-star restaurant. A must for serious foodies and lovers of high style.

Foley's on the Mall €€ *South Mall, Lismore, Co Waterford, tel: (058) 72511,* www.foleysonthemall.ie. Wed, Thurs, Fri, Sat & Sun 12.30–11.30pm. Gastropub in a historic building. Heated outdoor area with music in the Summer months. Good value for money with excellent service.

The Strand Inn €–€€ *Dunmore East, Co Waterford, tel: (051) 383 174,* www. thestrandinn.com. Breakfast and lunch from 8am until late. Situated beside a former smuggler's cove, this 300-year-old inn specialises in superb fresh seafood, seasonal produce and homemade desserts. There's also a lively pub with music.

The Tannery Restaurant €€€ *10 Quay Street, Dungarvan, tel: (058) 45420,* www. tannery.ie. Dinner Tues, Wed, Thurs, Fri & Sat 5.30–9pm, Sun 12.30–3.30pm. One of the country's most stylish gourmet restaurants in a converted leather warehouse. The chef's table menu option provides a dinner party experience for groups.

WEXFORD

Beaches at Kelly's Resort Hotel €€ *Rosslare, tel: (053) 913 2114,* www.kellys.ie. Daily 6.30–9pm. Reservations are essential at this firm favourite of locals and tourists alike. The food is delicious, and the wine list is enticing. Smart attire essential in the evening.

Dunbrody Country House Hotel €€€ *Arthurstown, New Ross, tel: (051) 389600,* www.dunbrodyhouse.com. Mon, Tues, Wed, Thurs, Fri & Sat 7–9.30pm, Sun 1.30–3.30pm. A blend of classical Irish cooking and continental charm served in the Harvest Room, which overlooks an organic vegetable and fruit garden.

Marlfield House Hotel €€ *Courtown Road, Gorey, tel: (053) 942 1124,* www.marlfieldhouse.com. *Thurs, Fri, Sat & Sun* 12–4pm, 5–9pm. The menu at The Duck Restaurant is modern fusion and Italian. Fresh herbs, vegetables, and fruit are picked from Marlfield's own gardens. A delightful experience.

WICKLOW

Darcy McGees €€ *Main Street, Arklow, tel: (0402) 91556,* www.darcymcgeesatthespawell.ie. Daily 12–9pm. A full carvery is available on a daily basis, as well as a wide array of sandwiches and an a la carte evening.

The Hungry Monk €€ *Church Road, Greystones, tel: (01) 201 0710,* www.thehungrymonk.ie. Wed, Thurs, Fri & Sat 5–11pm, Sun 12.30–8.30pm. Intimate, candlelit restaurant in a seaside village, specialising in seafood in summer and wild game in winter. Extensive wine list and craft beer menu. Lively fun atmosphere.

Hunter's Hotel €€–€€€ *Newrath Bridge, Rathnew, tel: (0404) 40106,* www.hunters.ie. Daily lunch 1–2.30pm, afternoon tea 4–5.30pm, dinner 7.30–9pm. Hunter's Hotel is an historic eighteenth-century coaching inn with fine gardens. The food here is simple but impressive traditional Irish fare.

The Roundwood Inn €€ *Roundwood, tel: (01) 281 8107,* www.roundwood.ie/dining. Daily noon–8.45pm. Atmospheric old inn serving local produce from lamb to venison. Good bar food, including goulash, Irish stew and smoked salmon. Reservations necessary for the restaurant.

NORTHERN IRELAND

Deane's Meat Locker £££ *28–40 Howard Street, Belfast BT1 6PF, tel: (028) 9033 1134*, www.michaeldeane.co.uk. Tues 5–9.30pm, Wed, Thurs & Fri 12–3pm, Sat 12–10pm. Deane's Restaurant offers one of the most memorable fine-dining experience in Belfast in striking minimalist surroundings.

Howard Street ££ *56 Howard Street, Belfast BT1 6PG, tel: (028) 9024 8362*, www.howardstbelfast.com. Tues, Wed, Thurs & Fri 5–9.30pm, Sat 2–9.30pm. Hip restaurant serving delicious locally sourced dishes.

House, Belfast £–££ *59-63 Botanic Avenue, Belfast BT7 1JL, tel: (028) 9531 3120*, www.housebelfast.co.uk. Wed noon–12am, Thurs & Fri 7am–12am, Sat & Sun 8am–12am. This lively boutique hotel, restaurant, and bar serves traditional Irish cuisine with a cosmopolitan twist. Conveniently located close to Queen's University. Vegetarian and gluten-free options.

The Percy French Pub and Bistro ££ *Hastings Slieve Donard Hotel, Downs Road, Newcastle, County Down BT33 0AH, tel: (028) 4372 3175*, www.hastings hotels.com. Daily noon–9.30pm. A welcoming and popular venue, serving pub lunch and dinner fare. More formal meals in the Oak Room.

Saltwater Brig ££ *43 Rowreagh Rd, Kircubbin, County Down BT22 1AR, tel: (028) 4273 8435* www.saltwaterbrig.com. Wed & Thurs 12–7.45pm, Fri & Sat 12–8.45pm, Sun 12–7.45pm. This family-run pub and restaurant has unbeatable views of Strangford Lough and the Mountains of Mourne. Traditional fare prepared with fresh, local ingredients. Sunday roast is very popular.

Shipquay Restaurant ££ *15/17 Shipquay Street, Derry BT48 6DJ, tel: (028) 712 67266*, www.shipquayhotel.com. Daily 8–10am, Sun, Mon, Tues, Wed & Thurs 5–9pm, Sat & Sun noon–4pm. Serving breakfasts, brunches and beautiful dinners seven days a week, from the midst of Derry's shopping and cultural hub. Classy and convivial, with a wide-ranging menu (including vegetarian options), using locally sourced ingredients, and a decent wine list.

TRAVEL ESSENTIALS

PRACTICAL INFORMATION

A

ACCOMMODATION (See also Camping, Youth Hostels, and the selection of Recommended Hotels starting on page 134)

While exploring Ireland you can stay in a wide range of accommodation: from luxury hotels to family-run guesthouses, to farmhouses and thatched cottages, to bed and breakfasts (B&Bs). Efficient tourist offices will handle both spur-of-the-moment or long-range reservations for you in tourist board-approved accommodation. Alternately, visit www.ireland.com or www.discoverireland.ie for accommodation offers and good-value inclusive packages. Tariffs are government-controlled, and the maximum rate which proprietors may charge is displayed in all hotel rooms.

Hotel bills sometimes include a service charge, and you will find that VAT (value added tax) on the total cost of accommodation, meals, and services is included in the rates.

Hotels and motels. These are graded by the tourist authorities into five-star ratings.

***** Most luxurious, highest standard of cuisine and services.

**** Extremely comfortable, with many amenities and fine dining.

*** Well-furnished, with private bath and many amenities.

** Well-kept, limited but good cuisine and service, most with private bath.

* Clean, comfortable, hot and cold running water, some en-suite facilities.

The Irish Hotels Federation (www.irelandhotels.com) and the Northern Ireland Hotels Federation (www.nihf.co.uk) list associated hotels. B&B Ireland (www.bandbireland.com) is the major association of bed and breakfast providers. The Irish Self-Catering Federation (www.iscf.ie) lists registered providers, including thatched cottages.

AIRPORTS

International flights arrive at Dublin, Cork, Shannon, Knock, and Belfast. Flights also operate from some UK airports to Kerry, Galway, Waterford, Donegal, City of Derry, and Sligo.

Dublin Airport, (DUB, tel: (01) 814 1111; www.dublinairport.com) 11km (7 miles) north of the Republic's capital, is the busiest. Aircoach provides air-conditioned coaches with free Wi-fi to the city centre, South Dublin, Bray, Greystones, Cork, and Belfast. For the best prices pre-book online, see www.aircoach.ie. However, you travel, the trip takes between half an hour and an hour. Taxi time between the airport and central Dublin is also about half an hour.

Shannon Airport (SNN, tel: (61) 712 000; www.shannonairport.com), one of the first trans-Atlantic gateways, is situated about 24km (15 miles) to the west of Limerick. JJ Kavanagh & Sons provide coaches to Limerick, Nenagh and Dublin Airport. Prices from €5, see http://jjkavanagh.ie.

Belfast International Airport (Aldergrove, BFS, tel: (028) 9448 4848; www.belfastairport.com) is 24km (15 miles) west of the city. A bus service to town operates every 30 minutes and costs £7.50. Airporter coaches link both of Belfast's airports with Derry, see http://airporter.co.uk. Prices start at £20.

George Best Belfast City Airport (BHD, tel: (028) 9093 9093; www.belfastcityairport.com) is handily situated near the city's old docklands, only 5km (3 miles) from Belfast City Centre. Buses run every 20 minutes and cost £2.50.

B

BICYCLE HIRE

Bikes are easy to rent. See www.discoverireland.ie/cycling for dealer contacts. The hugely popular dublinbikes (www.dublinbikes.ie) is a public bicycle hire scheme, which is free for the first 30 minutes.

BUDGETING FOR YOUR TRIP

Average prices in euros with British pounds where applicable.

Accommodation: (based on bed and breakfast in a standard double room in low–high seasons) luxury hotel over €200 (£150)–mid-range hotel €100–200 (£80–150); guesthouse/bed and breakfast €30–100 (£25–80).

Airport transfer: Dublin Airport to city centre by bus €7 (£5), by taxi €30 (£25) plus tip; Belfast International to city centre by bus €6, taxi £25; Belfast City Airport to city centre by bus £2.50, taxi £8.

Bicycle rental: about €75 (£60 per week, plus deposit).

Buses: local fares €4.30 (to the most distant suburb). An eight-day out of 16 Open-Road pass (bus only, longer and shorter options available) covering the Republic of Ireland is €142.50 (www.buseireann.ie). A five-day Tourist Rambler bus ticket for the greater Dublin area costs €33, while a 30-day ticket is €165 (www.dublinbus.ie). Belfast Metro bus fares start from £2 for short journeys within the city up to £15 for a Smartlink Card giving you up to 10 journeys within the city and its outskirts.

Camping: around €9 (£7) per person per night for a tent pitch.

Entertainment: Cinema tickets cost around €10 (£7.3). Admission prices for nightclubs are €/£5–20 or more. Theatre tickets are €15–60 (£13–50).

Ferry: Galway–Aran Islands €25 roundtrip.

Meals and drinks: Expect to pay €25–65 (£20–54) per person for dinner with wine and coffee; up to €5.50 (£4.80) for a pint of Guinness, €5 (£4) for a pint of beer.

Museums, stately homes: €5–12 (£4.30–10).

Taxis: two-mile taxi journey in Dublin €10. You may find a supplement is payable for extra passengers, baggage, etc.

Tours: Dublin hop-on, hop-off bus tour €15-20. Bus tour around Ring of Kerry from Killarney €25. Belfast City Black Taxi Tour, £25 for up to two people (75 mins).

Trains: Dublin–Cork from €78 return.

C

CAMPING

Officially-approved campsites range from basic to luxurious. Many a farmer will let campers stay on his property, but always ask first. Hiring camper vans is increasingly popular, see www.bunkcampers.com. If you are bringing your own caravan, note that the connections for Calor gas tanks are not compatible with the cylinders sold in Ireland. Lists of camping and caravanning parks and their facilities are available from tourist information offices or the Irish Caravan and Camping Council (www.camping-ireland.ie). Contact the Northern Ireland Tourist Board; tel: (028) 9023 1221; www.discovernorthern ireland.com.

Horse-drawn caravans, most commonly found in west and southwest Ireland, can be rented by the week to sample the gypsy life. Book in advance through www.irishhorsedrawncaravans.com.

CAR HIRE (See also Driving in Ireland)

Car rental companies operate at airports and in towns. International firms usually have slightly higher rates than their local competitors. Some companies permit cars to be picked up in one place and returned elsewhere.

Most companies have a two-tiered tariff, raising prices by up to 20 percent for the summer season. In any season, cars may be rented on either a time-plus-mileage basis or with unlimited mileage, but if you're unsure whether you'll be chalking up enough travelling to justify the unlimited rate, the firm may agree to let you choose the more favourable tariff retroactively. Investigate before you travel.

A valid national licence, normally at least two years old, is required. Many car rental companies permit 21-year-old drivers to hire cars, but the minimum age can be up to 25. The maximum age, depending on the company, ranges from 65 to 70. Credit cards are usually the preferred means of payment.

Rentals begin at around €25 (£18.5) per day or €135 (£100) per week for a small car, including third party insurance, unlimited mileage and taxes. Add about €10 per day for collision damage waiver. Additional coverage can be arranged on the spot, and comprehensive coverage is recommended.

CLIMATE AND CLOTHING

The Gulf Stream is credited with keeping the Irish weather mild year-round, but the unexpected can happen with readings as cold as -19°C (-2°F) and as hot as 33°C (92°F) recorded over the past century. May is usually the sunniest

month of the year, and December the dullest.
Average monthly temperatures in Dublin:

	J	F	M	A	M	J	J	A	S	O	N	D
°F	41	41	43	47	51	56	59	58	56	50	45	43
°C	5	5	6	8	11	13	15	14	13	10	7	6

Temperatures do not vary much from north to south, but the weather in the west and southwest can be a good deal wetter than elsewhere because the winds come in direct from the sea. Pack some light protective clothing for the summer, and warmer items in the winter.

In the winter the Wicklow Mountains near Dublin, Donegal in the northwest and County Kerry in the southwest have heavy snowfalls, making the territory dangerous even for seasoned walkers and climbers. Wear warm, protective clothing, inform the hotel owners of your route and time of return and take some provisions with you.

CRIME (See also Emergencies and Police)

The Crime Prevention Office of the Garda Siochana (police) warns visitors to carry a minimum of cash and jewellery. Pickpockets do operate in shops and public places. Park in well-lit, busy areas. The Irish Tourist Assistance Service (ITAS) supports tourists who have been the victim of crime, see http://itas.ie.

D

DRIVING (See also Car Rental and Emergencies)

Drive on the left and give way to traffic from the right.

Taking your own car. Be sure to have the registration papers and insurance coverage. Virtually any valid driving licence from any country is recognised in

Ireland. If yours doesn't include a photograph, keep your passport with you when driving.

Speed limits. Unless otherwise marked, the speed limit in the Irish Republic is 50kmh (30mph) in towns, 80kmh (50mph) on local roads, 100kmh (62mph) on national roads and dual carriageways and 120kmh (74mph) on motorways. In Northern Ireland: 30mph (50kmh) in towns, 60mph (86kmh) on local roads, and 70mph (44kmh) on national roads, dual carriageways and motorways.

Fuel. In some areas finding a petrol station open on a Sunday morning may be a problem, so it's best to top up on Saturday for weekend excursions. Petrol (gas) is sold by the litre.

Seat belts. Drivers and front-seat passengers must wear seat belts in the Republic and Northern Ireland; failure to use them may be punished by a fine. If a vehicle is built with rear seat belts, it is compulsory to use them.

Drinking and driving. Random breath tests are used in certain areas. Those who fail risk heavy fines or jail or both. This affects visitors as well as residents.

Road signs. The road direction signs in the Republic are mostly bilingual, in English and Gaelic. Road signs give distances in kilometres in the Republic and miles in Northern Ireland.

E

ELECTRICITY

The standard current everywhere is 220v, 50AC, but you will find that hotels usually have special sockets for shavers, running at both 220 and 110v.

It is possible for certain appliances to need a converter, and also adapter plugs may be required to fit into Ireland's two types of wall outlets. These can be either three-pin flat or two-pin round.

EMBASSIES AND CONSULATES

Australia: 47–49 St Stephen's Green, Dublin 2; tel: (01) 664 5300; www. ireland.embassy.gov.au

Canada: 7–8 Wilton Terrace, Dublin 2; tel: (01) 234 4000; www.canada.ie
Great Britain: 29 Merrion Road, Dublin 4; tel: (01) 205 3700; www.british embassyinireland.fco.gov.uk
US: 42 Elgin Road, Dublin 4; tel: (01) 668 8777; https://ie.usembassy.gov
In Northern Ireland:
US: Danesfort House, 223 Stranmillis Road, Belfast BT9 5GR; tel: (028) 9038 6100; https://uk.usembassy.gov/embassy-consulates/belfast/

EMERGENCIES (See also Embassies and Health)

To contact the police, fire department, or an ambulance in the Republic or Northern Ireland, dial **999 or 112** and tell the emergency operator which service you need. Have details of your location ready before you make your call.

G

GETTING THERE

Visitors should note any current travel restrictions in place before travelling to Ireland.

From Great Britain
By Air
Visitors and tourists can fly in from airports across the UK to Dublin, Shannon, Cork, Kerry, Galway, Waterford, Donegal, Sligo, and Knock in the Republic and to Belfast International, George Best Belfast City, and Derry airports in Northern Ireland. New routes are opening all the time, so it may be worth checking with the airline of your choice for information on the most convenient connections.

Charter Flights and Package Tours. Some airlines offer fly-drive tours, as well as special fares which may include your flight and all the transport to and from your final destination in Ireland. Check with the airline of your choice.

Regional Flights. If your time in Ireland is short, you may consider domestic flights between regions. These are operated by Aer Lingus, tel: 1890 800 600 (Ireland) or 0333 004 5000 (UK).

By Sea

Passenger and car ferries sail frequently from Britain to Ireland. There are services from: Holyhead to Dublin, Liverpool, and Isle of Man to Dublin and Belfast, Fishguard, and Pembroke to Rosslare, Cairnryan, and Troon (Scotland) to Larne (near Belfast) and Stranraer to Belfast.

The main ferry operators include Irish Ferries (www.irishferries.com), P&O Irish Sea, Stena Line (www.stenaline.co.uk), and Steam Packet Company (www.steam-packet.com). Schedules, fares and contact numbers are posted on the companies' websites. Pets travelling to Ireland or Northern Ireland from the UK require a microchip, valid rabies vaccination, an animal health certificate or a pet passport issued in an EU country or Northern Ireland, and dogs require a tapeworm treatment.

From North America By Air

Travellers from almost every major American city and several major Canadian cities can make connections to Dublin, Shannon, Belfast, or Knock, either direct, or via New York, Chicago or Boston.

Charter Flights and Package Tours. Charter flights to Shannon, with connections to Dublin, feature even further air-fare reductions.

GUIDES AND TOURS

Guided tours are conducted at some major attractions as part of the admission fee, and a variety of excursions are led by guides, covering major monuments and beauty spots by bus. Tourist offices have schedules. The Tourist Office Dublin at 37 College Green, Dublin 2, tel: (01) 410 0700, www.tourist officedublin.com and **Fáilte Ireland** (the National Tourist Development Authority) at 88/95 Amiens Street, Dublin 1, tel: (01) 884 7101, www.failteireland. ie have a list of qualified guides. See also www.discoverireland.ie.

H

HEALTH AND MEDICAL CARE (See also Emergencies)

Residents of EU countries are covered by reciprocal health care in the Republic and in Northern Ireland, and visitors should be sure to bring their European

Health Insurance Card (EHIC). For UK citizens an existing EHIC will remain valid until the expiry date on the card. The UK Global Health Insurance Card (UK GHIC) will replace the EHIC for most people. Other nationalities should have some form of medical insurance – most travel insurance policies provide adequate cover.

Hotels and pharmacies usually know which local doctors are available, but in an emergency dial **999** or **112** to find a doctor on call. VHI Swift Care Clinics (tel: 1890 866 966; www.vhi.ie/swiftcare) provide walk-in urgent care centres in Dublin and Cork. The Dental Hospital (20 Lincoln Place, Dublin 2, tel: (01) 612 7200, www.dentalhospital.ie), will treat emergency cases.

Pharmacies (chemists) operate during shopping hours. A few stay open until 10pm; in Belfast many are open on Sundays, while in the Republic only some are open for limited hours.

L

LANGUAGE

English is spoken everywhere in Ireland. In the Gaeltacht areas of the west and south, the principal language is Irish, though everyone can speak English too. Bilingualism is officially encouraged. For short language learning courses in the Gaeltacht, try www.gael-linn.ie or www.liofa.eu.

Here is a short Irish glossary to help you read the signs:

Irish/Gaelic English

Áth ford of river

baile/bally hamlet, group of houses, town

beann/ben mountain peak

cairn mound of stones atop a prehistoric tomb

carrick/carrig rock

cather fort

clachan/clochan small group of dwellings; stepping stones across a river; beehive-shaped hut

corrach marsh or low plain

derry/dare oak tree or wood

donagh church

drum/drom ridge, hillock
dun/doon fort
ennis/inch, innis(h) island
kil, kill, cill church; monk's cell
lough lake, sea inlet
sceillig/skellig crag, rock
sliabh/slieve mountain
tulach/tully hillock

Here are some handy phrases, with a rough guide to pronunciation:

Dia dhuit *diah guich* hello
Slán *slawn* goodbye
oiche mhaith *e-ha wah* good night
go raibh maith agat *goh rev moh a-gut* thank you
le do thoil *leh doh hol* please
tá fáilte romhat *taw faltcha rowet* you're welcome
sláinte! *sloyn-tcha!* cheers!
gabh mo leithscéal *gaw mah leshkale* excuse me
Cá bhfuil an ... ? *koh will on … ?* Where is the ... ?
fir/mná *fear/min-aw* men/women

LGBTQ TRAVELLERS

Typically people in Ireland are very open and friendly and accepting towards LGBTQ travellers. Attitudes in the more remote areas of the country (and some fundamentalist enclaves in the North) can be considerably more conservative, but overall viewpoints have changed enormously in recent decades and the country was the first in the world to leagalise same-sex marriage by popular vote in 2015.

There are a smattering of gay bars and clubs on offer in the bigger cities.

Various organisations provide LGBTQ advisory services. They include the **Gay Switchboard** (www.gayswitchboard.ie), and the Dublin-based **Lesbian Line** (www.dublinlesbianline.ie). **TENI** - Transgender Equality Network Ireland offers (www.teni.ie) a range of support services to the transgender community.

M

MEDIA

Radio and Television. In the Republic, state-run Radio Telefís Éireann (RTE) is the largest broadcaster, though cable and digital television has expanded the choice and includes standard British stations. Most programmes are in English except for a few Irish or bilingual ones. RTE operates three radio stations mainly in English, TG4 in Irish, as well as Raidió na Gaeltachta with an all-Irish programme. In Northern Ireland, the BBC runs five radio stations and two TV stations alongside ITV and Channel Four.

Newspapers. Popular daily broadsheets are the *Irish Independent*, the *Irish Times* and the *Irish Examiner* and, in Northern Ireland, the *News Letter* and the *Belfast Telegraph*.

Entertainment news is covered in the *Herald* of Dublin, the *Evening Echo* of Cork and the *Belfast Telegraph*. Sunday papers, such as the Sunday Independent, are also useful, and visitors will find a what's on section in the Friday edition of the *Irish Times*.

Irish editions of Britain's national daily and Sunday newspapers are sold almost everywhere in both countries on the morning of publication. Leading newsagents in the major towns also sell international newspapers and magazines.

MONEY

Currency. The unit of currency used in the Irish Republic is the euro (€); in Northern Ireland the British pound sterling (£) is used. Both are divided into 100 units. These units are called cents in the Republic, pence in the north. Euro banknotes are issued in €5, €10, €20, €50, €100 and also €500 denominations. Coins come in 1, 2, 5, 10, 20 and 50 cents and 1 and 2 euro.

Exchange facilities. All major banks and many building societies provide exchange facilities. Major post offices, including the GPO in Dublin, have a bureau de change. Some international travel agencies also change money and travellers' cheques. Be sure to bring photo ID when cashing travellers' cheques.

The Suffolk Street Dublin Tourism Office and Visit Belfast Welcome Centre

on Donegall Square North operate money exchange services.
Credit cards are widely accepted.

OPENING HOURS

The opening hours of shops and offices can vary from season to season and according to where they are located.

Shops in the cities are normally open from 9am–6pm Mon–Sat and often on Sunday afternoons; country towns have one early closing day. Big shopping centres often stay open until 9pm on Thu and Fri. Smaller shops, particularly grocers and newsagents, often open on Sun and many stay open until 11pm.

Offices and businesses mostly operate from 9am–5.30pm Mon–Fri. Tourist information offices usually open from 9 or 10am–5pm with longer summer hours in the busiest places.

Banks. In general banks open 9.30am–4pm Mon to Fri in the Republic. Most towns have a late opening day once a week (Thurs in Dublin), when banks open until 5pm. Most remain open over the lunch hour. Northern Ireland banks have similar opening hours, although outside Belfast, branches may close for lunch.

Pubs. In the Republic, the hours are generally 10.30am–11.30pm during the week, with an extra hour Thurs–Sat. On Sunday they can open at noon and stop serving at 11pm. In addition, there is half an hour drinking up time in the evenings all year round. All pubs are closed, by law, on Christmas Day and Good Friday. Licensing laws in Northern Ireland were changed in 2021. Pubs in Northern Ireland can apply to serve alcohol until 2am (BST). Restrictions on late openings on Sundays were removed. Drinking up time in the north is one hour.

Museums and stately homes. Museums and stately homes follow no general rule except that visiting hours will often be curtailed in winter. There are no universal days when these institutions are closed, though Sun, Mon, or Tues are the most probable. To avoid disappointment always check first with the nearest tourist information office.

P

PHOTOGRAPHY

Be sure to ask permission before you take photos in museums and historic churches; sometimes flash is forbidden. Military bases (and installations of security forces in Northern Ireland) are off-limits to photographers.

POLICE (See also Emergencies)

The civic guard (police force) of the Irish Republic is the Garda Siochana, known as the Garda (pronounced 'gorda'). The Police Service of Northern Ireland performs similar duties in the North. In case of emergency, telephone 999 or 112, in both the Republic and Northern Ireland.

POST OFFICES

An Post operates all mail services offered in the Republic. Most mailboxes are pillar-shaped and painted green. Most post offices are open from 9am–5.30pm, but the main one – the historic General Post Office in O'Connell Street, Dublin – is open Mon–Sat 8.30am–6pm. Smaller post offices close from 1pm–2pm. Postcard shops and newsstands sometimes sell stamps too. In some areas a post office may be identified by a sign in Irish only – *Oifig an Phoist*.

In Northern Ireland the mailboxes are red. Note that Republic of Ireland stamps may not be used on mail posted in Northern Ireland and British stamps are invalid in the Republic.

PUBLIC HOLIDAYS

Banks and businesses are closed on public holidays, though some shops and restaurants may stay open. If a date falls on a Sunday, then the following Monday is taken in lieu.

In the Republic of Ireland and Northern Ireland:
1 January New Year's Day
17 March St. Patrick's Day

March/April (movable date) Good Friday/Easter Monday
first Monday in May May Day
25 December Christmas Day
26 December Boxing Day
In the Republic of Ireland only:
first Monday in June June Bank Holiday
first Monday in August August Bank Holiday
last Monday in October October Bank Holiday
In Northern Ireland only:
last Monday in May Spring Bank Holiday
12 July Orangemen's Day
last Monday in August Summer Bank Holiday

R

RELIGION

About 87 percent of the people in the Irish Republic are Catholic. A declining number go to Sunday Mass, which can be heard in Dublin and elsewhere any time from 6am–9pm. Dublin's cathedrals are (Anglican) Church of Ireland, and schedules of the services at these and other Protestant churches can be found in hotels, and in Saturday papers. Dublin has Protestant, Greek Orthodox, Jewish, Islamic, Hindu, Buddhist, and Sikh places of worship.

In Northern Ireland, Catholics make up just under half of the population, outnumbering the largest single Protestant group, the Presbyterians, as well as the Church of Ireland and the Methodist church. The ecclesiastic capital of Ireland is Armagh, situated in the North with two cathedrals, one Catholic and the other Church of Ireland. Both are called St Patrick's.

T

TELEPHONES

Public telephones are increasingly rare but can still be found in post offices, hotels, stores and on the street. They are marked in Gaelic, *Telefon*. In Northern

Ireland, public telephones are found in metal and glass booths or yellow cubicles. They also generally accept coins and cards.

Most payphones in Ireland take pre-paid phone cards from local post offices and shops. Dial 10 for operator assistance.

Only mobiles with multi-band GSM will work in Ireland. If your phone is non-GSM contact your provider before travelling. It may be cheaper to buy a local SIM card and top up with prepaid calls. If you are coming from the UK your mobile should work in Northern Ireland. You will need international roaming in the Republic.

The international dialling code for the Republic of Ireland is 353 – drop the initial zero of the local STD code or mobile number. Northern Ireland is 44 as it is part of the UK. The local code for Northern Ireland is 028, from the Republic you can dial 00 44 28 or simply dial 048 followed by the eight-digit number.

TIME ZONES

Ireland sets its clocks one hour ahead of GMT from mid-March to the end of October, but the rest of the year the clocks are set to GMT.

TIPPING

Some hotels and restaurants include a service charge, so tipping is unnecessary. If not, 10 percent of the bill in a restaurant and a couple of euros a day for cleaners is expected in both the Republic and Northern Ireland. Taxis are usually tipped by simply rounding up the fare.

TOILETS

Gender signs on doors in the Republic may be printed in Gaelic, not English. *Mná* is Gaelic for ladies; *fir* means gentlemen.

TOURIST INFORMATION OFFICES

Tourist information offices and Discover Ireland Centres all over Ireland provide full travel information and advice, booklets, maps and a comprehensive hotel reservation service (for a small charge). The offices are usually open from 9 or 10am–5 or 6pm, although many local ones operate only in the summer.

For enquiries, contact:

Fáilte Ireland (the National Tourist Development Authority), 88-95 Amiens Street, Dublin 1, tel: (01) 884 7101, www.failteireland.ie, www.discoverireland.ie.

Northern Ireland Tourist Board, St Anne's Court, 59 North Street, Belfast BT1 INB; tel: (028) 9023 1221; www.discovernorthernireland.com. You may also address your enquiries to offices of the **British Tourist Authority** the world over, www.visitbritain.com.

TRANSPORT

Buses. The state-run Bus Éireann operates an extensive network of local, provincial, and express bus routes in the Republic, including full cross-border services in conjunction with Northern Ireland's Ulsterbus Ltd. Services to tourist destinations increases in summer. Fares and schedule information can be downloaded from www.buseireann.ie. Expressway buses provide a non-stop inter-city service, while Provincial vehicles make frequent stops in rural areas.

Dublin Bus *(Bus Atha Cliath)* runs services in the Dublin area. For information, tel: (01) 873 4222, www.dublinbus.ie. Dublin Area Rapid Transit (DART) provides a swift and frequent rail link through the city, from Howth in the north to Greystones in the south. For information on fares and schedules, see www.irishrail.ie/dart. The Luas tram system also provides light rail service to outlying suburbs, tel: 1850 300 604, www.luas.ie.

Bus Éireann sell Open Road passes – allowing flexible cross-country travel for varying periods – eg three days out of six, right up to 15 days out of 30. There is also a Rover ticket, which allows up to 15 days of unlimited travel in the Republic, and includes the use of Ulsterbus in Northern Ireland. Or you can buy tickets for combined bus and rail travel: the Explorer pass, for example, is valid in the Republic only.

Trains. Cross-country services to and from Dublin are both quick and comfortable. The main inter-city routes have air-conditioned, sound-proofed expresses. City Gold (First Class) is only available on intercity Dublin-Cork trains and the Dublin-Belfast route has First Plus. Irish Rail *(Iarnród Éireann)* operates trains in the Republic; tel: (1850) 366 222, www.irishrail.ie. In Northern Ireland, Translink operates Northern Ireland Railways, Enterprise (Belfast–Dublin train service), Ulsterbus (inter-urban), Metro bus (Belfast City) and Goldline (coach); tel: (028) 9066 6630; www.translink.co.uk. Train timetables are available at railway stations and tourist offices, and are also posted on the rail companies' websites.

Note: Dublin has two main-line railway stations (Heuston and Connolly), as well as a commuter-line station, so be sure to check in advance for the correct terminal.

Travellers can use the **Eurail Pass** in Ireland, a flat-rate unlimited mileage ticket, valid for rail travel in Europe outside the UK and also the new Eurail Global Pass, which includes countries worldwide. Saver versions are available for those under 26.

Taxis. Most taxis park at designated stands waiting for clients. Many towns have radio-dispatched taxis or online booking, but these usually charge extra for the mileage to pick up the client. Fares can vary from town to town. Dublin and Cork have metered taxis while smaller towns have standard fares or charges by agreement.

Note that you should pay only the charge on the meter plus, if applicable, supplements for extra passengers, additional luggage, waiting time, and trips on public holidays or after midnight. An appropriate tip will be appreciated. Detailed receipts will be provided on request.

Boats and Ferries. With over 4,800km (3,000 miles) of coastline and 14,480km (9,000 miles) of rivers and streams, Ireland is a boater's paradise. You might rent a fishing boat to take advantage of the excellent fresh-water and sea fishing, or enjoy the country's scenic splendours in a rented cruiser (normally available with two to eight berths).

No boating permit is needed for travelling on the Shannon, and all companies offer a free piloting lesson. Points of departure include Carrick-on-Shannon, Athlone, Banagher and Killaloe.

The rugged islands off the coast of Ireland are rich in folklore, antiquities and eye-catching natural wonders (especially birdlife). Fáilte Ireland produces a free brochure, *Explore Islands of Ireland* listing numerous possibilities, including scheduled ferries. This information can also be found at www.discover ireland.ie.

The Aran Islands are only a 20km (30mile) steamer ride from the Galway coast at Rossaveal, and crossings can also be made in May to September from Doolin in County Clare. Garinish Island, which is noted for its exuberant vegetation, is only ten minutes away from Glengarriff (County Cork).

Bad weather may interrupt ferry services. There are connections to the Aran Islands by air, as well; flights take around ten minutes.

TRAVELLERS WITH DISABILITIES

A lot of progress has been made in recent years to provide more facilities for travellers with disabilities. Ramps have been provided, giving access to many community buildings, and much of the public transport system has been adapted. The more modern buses in Dublin have facilities for wheelchair users, and trains have level entry access. The Accessible Ireland website lists attractions which are wheelchair friendly, see www.accessible ireland.com.

V

VISAS AND ENTRY REQUIREMENTS

Citizens of many countries do not require visas. EU citizens can enter with a valid passport or national ID card. UK nationals are advised to travel with a passport as an immigration officer may ask for proof that you are a UK citizen with Common Travel Area rights. See www.dfa.ie for further information on entry requirements.

If you are coming from outside the euro zone, you must fill in a Customs declaration form for cash sums of over €10,000.

The customs restrictions between the Republic and Northern Ireland are normally limited to animals and agricultural products. There are no longer any border security checkpoints but there are selective checks carried out by customs officers. This may all change in the event of Brexit.

For further customs regulations information, visit www.revenue.ie.

W

WEBSITES

http://entertainment.ie Find out what's going on.
www.discovernorthernireland.com Northern Ireland Tourist Board.
www.heritageireland.ie Heritage of Ireland.
www.discoverireland.ie Ireland's National Tourism Board.
www.ireland.com Reserve hotels and explore Ireland.
www.visitdublin.com Dublin's official travel and tourism site.
www.visitbelfast.com Official Belfast tourist information.
www.ringofkerrytourism.com The Ring of Kerry: hotels, activities

Y

YOUTH HOSTELS

The Irish Youth Hostels Association runs 24 hostels in the Republic of Ireland. Membership cards are required to be able to use them, which are issued by national youth hostel associations overseas. **Independent Hostels of Ireland,** (tel: (74) 973 0130 for a brochure or see www.independent hostelsireland.com) is an association of hostel owners with no membership or age requirements and no curfew. There are some 70 hostels throughout Ireland.

There are six youth hostels in Northern Ireland. Ask for details from **Hostelling International Northern Ireland**, 22–32 Donegall Road, Belfast BT12 5JN; tel: (028) 9032 4733; www.hini.org.uk.

WHERE TO STAY

Price categories below are for a standard double room in high season (some include breakfast – check when you book). Please bear in mind that prices can be much cheaper and deals are often available:

€€€	over €200	£££	over £150
€€	€100–200	££	£80–150
€	under €100	£	under £80

DUBLIN

Aberdeen Lodge €€ *53-55 Park Avenue, Dublin 4, tel: (01) 283 8155, www. aberdeen-lodge.com.* A large Victorian house in the elegant embassy quarter with quiet, spacious bedrooms, beautifully furnished. A five-minute bus or DART ride to the city centre.

Blooms Hotel €–€€ *6 Anglesea Street, Dublin 2, tel: (01) 671 5622, www. blooms.ie.* Located in the Temple Bar area, and like most hotels here, there's a stylish restaurant, bar, and basement nightclub to keep you entertained most of the night.

Buswells Hotel €€ *23–27 Molesworth Street, Dublin 2, tel: (01) 614 6500, www. buswells.ie.* Centrally located just opposite the National Museums complex, Buswells is set in a former Georgian townhouse and a favourite haunt of Dublin politicians. Most come just for the restaurant and bar.

Central Hotel €–€€ *1–5 Exchequer Street, Dublin 2, tel: (01) 679 7302, www. centralhoteldublin.com.* Around for over 100 years and housed in a rambling, refurbished Victorian building with a location as central as its name. The first floor Library Bar attracts literary types.

Clarence Hotel €€€ *6–8 Wellington Quay, Dublin 2, tel: (01) 407 0800, www. theclarence.ie.* Once upon a time this was simply a home for clergy up from the country on business. Since being bought, refurbished (and later sold) by Bono and the Edge from U2, its Octagon bar is one of the most popular meeting places in Dublin. The hotel itself is decked out with Irish craftsmanship that's contemporary yet reminiscent of the country's past.

Clayton Hotel Ballsbridge €€ *Merrion Road, Dublin 4, tel: (01) 668 1111, www.claytonhotels.com.* An excellent value hotel next to the RDS Arena with over 300 rooms at a flat rate, and a lively lounge bar. Ample car parking onsite, and a five-minute bus or DART ride to the city.

Conrad Dublin €€€ *Earlsfort Terrace, Dublin 2, tel: (01) 602 8900, www.hilton.com.* Situated just off St Stephen's Green, the Conrad is the first stop for travelling royalty, though the service seems to roll out the red carpet for all guests. It's most popular for business people but the pub attracts Dubliners.

Jacobs Inn € *21 – 28 Talbot Pl, Mountjoy, Dublin 1 (01) 855 5660, http://jacobs inn.com.* Bright and friendly budget accommodation, situated among casual Irish pubs and Georgian architecture.

The Morrison €€€ *Lower Ormond Quay, Dublin 1, tel: (01) 887 2400, www.morrisonhotel.ie.* City-centre quayside hotel (a Doubletree by Hilton) that vies with the Clarence (see above) for title of hippest hotel in town. Contemporary design and good location.

Davenport Hotel €€–€€€ *Merrion Square, Dublin 2, tel: (01) 607 3500, http://davenporthotel.ie.* An elegant lemon-coloured building dating from the 1860s set amidst the attractions of Merrion Square.

The Shelbourne €€€ *27 St Stephen's Green, Dublin 2, tel: (01) 663 4500, www.theshelbourne.ie.* Once home to the Irish Constitution (it was written here), the Shelbourne now hosts Dublin's more affluent visitors. You couldn't ask for more than a room overlooking St Stephen's Green, but the popularity of the Horseshoe Bar with Dublin's glitterati will give you even more to look at.

Staunton's on the Green €€ *83 St Stephen's Green South, Dublin 2, tel: (01) 478 2300, www.stauntonsonthegreen.ie.* Exclusive Georgian guesthouse overlooking the green with spacious rooms and delightful period decor.

The Westbury €€€ *Balfe Street, Dublin 2, tel: (01) 679 1122*, www.doyle collection.com. A luxury city centre hotel that knows best how to cater to business visitors, though with this location (just off Grafton St) sight-seeing travellers won't need to walk far to the city's attractions.

Wynn's Hotel €€ *35–39 Lower Abbey Street, Dublin 1, tel: (01) 874 5131*, www.wynnshotel.ie. This centrally-located hotel is just around the corner from the Abbey Theatre.

The Marker Hotel €€€ *Grand Canal Square, Dublin 2, tel (01) 687 5100*, www.themarkerhoteldublin.com. The newest addition to Dublin's luxury hotel scene is slap bang in the middle of the docklands, opposite the Grand Canal Theatre. The building is unapologetically modernist and sleek. Head to the rooftop bar for panoramic views of the city.

MEATH

The Millhouse €€€ *Slane, County Meath, tel: (041) 982 0878*, www.themillhouse.ie. Romantic Georgian manor with sumptuous four posters, log fires and the beautiful River Boyne as a backdrop.

CORK

Bellinter House €€€ *Navan, County Meath, tel: (046) 903 0900*, www.bellinterhouse.com. Luxury boutique hotel in a magnificent eighteenth-century country house, set in extensive grounds. Awarding-winning spa and gourmet dining in a cool, informal atmosphere.

The Address €€ *Military Hill, St Luke's, Cork, tel: (021) 453 9000*, www.theaddresscork.com. An imposing Victorian building converted into a stylish, hill-top hotel, with great views of the city and harbour. Both bar and restaurant have a lively local trade.

Ballymaloe House €€€ *Shangarry, Midleton, tel: (021) 465 2531*, www.ballymaloe.ie. One of Ireland's leading country-house hotels, Ballymaloe is a stylishly decorated Georgian house surrounded by the family farm. Renowned for its restaurant, children welcome.

Blue Haven Hotel €€ *3 Pearse Street, Kinsale, tel: (021) 477 2209,* www.blue havenkinsale.com. The hotel's individually-styled rooms are well planned but compact, with the type of space you'd expect in a city centre hotel. There is a fine bar and coffee shop to retire to, and the location couldn't be better.

Seaview House Hotel €€ *Ballylickey, Bantry Bay, tel: (027) 50073,* www.sea viewhousehotel.com. Set in extensive grounds on the shores of Bantry Bay, this Victorian manor house is now a comfortable, family run, country house hotel, with an excellent restaurant. A good base for touring the Southwest.

GALWAY

The G Hotel €€€ *Wellpark, Galway, tel: (091) 865200,* www.theghotel.ie. Milliner Philip Treacy has designed a hotel that, like his hats, is quirky, extravagant, and luxurious. Kick back in the cool restaurant and bar or chill out in the soothing spa.

The Hardiman €€–€€€ *Eyre Square, Galway, tel: (091) 564041,* www.the hardiman.ie. Historic nineteenth-century railway hotel located in the heart of the city. There's no lack of old Irish charm here but a swish new makeover means it draws a trendy crowd these days. The Oyster Bar has a wide selection of drinks and an impressive cocktail list.

KERRY

Abbeyglen Castle Hotel €€ *Sky Road, Clifden, Co Galway, tel: (091) 21201,* www.abbeyglen.ie. Stay in an eccentric Irish castle with a parrot presiding over reception. Traditional Irish welcome with great food, a lively bar, and a sense of fun throughout.

Greenmount House €€ *Upper John Street, Dingle, tel: (066) 915 1414,* www. greenmounthouse.ie. Only a short walk from the busy town centre, this quiet fourteen-room guesthouse has a great view of the sunset over Dingle. Rooms are spacious and contemporary, and the breakfast is renowned.

Lake Hotel €–€€ *Muckross Road, Killarney, tel: (064) 663 1035,* www.lakehotel killarney.com. The grounds of this large, rambling, country hotel run right down to the lakeshore and adjoin Killarney National Park, putting you right in the middle of the Killarney experience. There's an outdoor hot tub on the lakeshore, which is part of a fitness centre.

Parknasilla Resort €€€ *Sneem, Ring of Kerry, tel: (064) 667 5600,* www.park nasillahotel.ie. Set in a sheltered inlet, with sub-tropical vegetation and a mountain backdrop, this is the ultimate getaway. Excellent pool and spa, old-fashioned lounge and bar, and self-catering options for families.

Sheen Falls Lodge €€€ *Kenmare, tel: (064) 664 1600,* www.sheenfallslodge. ie. A 120-hectare (300-acre) estate and waterside setting comes along with a room in this lodge. The lounge bar welcomes you in with a roaring fire and gives you a view of the spilling waterfall outside. Spacious rooms offer views of the river or Kenmare Bay. There is also an equestrian centre, library and nature walk through the woodland.

KILKENNY

Club House Hotel €€ *Patrick Street, Kilkenny, tel: (056) 772 1994,* www.club househotel.com. Historic eighteenth-century hotel; mementoes include a set of witty nineteenth-century political cartoons.

Hotel Kilkenny €€–€€€ *College Road, Kilkenny, tel: (056) 776 2000,* www.hotel kilkenny.ie. Hotel just outside the city with bedrooms, including some family rooms, in a light, contemporary design.

LIMERICK AND SHANNON

Carlton Castletroy Park Hotel €€–€€€ *Dublin Road, Limerick, tel: (061) 335566,* www.castletroypark.ie. One of Limerick's most sought-after hotels for conference facilities, but still capable of rolling out a proper welcome to recreational guests. Enjoy some relaxation at the Aqua and Fitness club or pamper yourself at the Blue Door Salon.

Dromoland Castle €€€ *Newmarket-on-Fergus, County Clare, tel: (061) 368144,* www.dromoland.ie. This luxury estate can trace its heritage back to Gaelic royalty via the O'Briens, once barons of Inchiquin, who were direct descendants of Brian Boru. The hotel is welcoming, relaxing, and steeped in history – especially the grounds which include a lake and delightful parklands.

Fitzgerald's Woodlands House Hotel €–€€ *Knockanes, Adare, County Limerick, tel: (061) 605100, www.woodlands-hotel.ie.* A lively, modern hotel just outside the village, this is a good base for touring the Shannon region. There's a new leisure centre and spa, and a choice of two popular restaurants.

Gregan's Castle €€€ *Ballyvaughan, County Clare, tel: (065) 707 7005, www.gregans.ie.* One of Ireland's leading country house hotels, with extensive gardens and breathtaking views over Galway Bay. Antique furniture, contemporary art, and an outstanding restaurant.

Sleepzone € *The Burren, Doolin Road, Lisdoonvarna, County Clare, tel: (065) 707 4036, www.sleepzone.ie.* A comfortable good value hostel, housed in a former hotel, in the lively village of Lisdoonvarna.

MAYO

Ashford Castle €€€ *Cong, County Mayo, tel: (094) 954 6003, www.ashfordcastle.com.* The last word in luxury accommodation, this former nineteenth-century Guinness family mansion is arguably Ireland's grandest castle hotel, with some parts dating back to the early thirteenth century. The best rooms are at the top of the castle and offer views of Lough Corrib, the River Cong, and the surrounding parkland.

Boffin Lodge € *The Quay, Westport, tel: (098) 26092, www.boffinlodge.com.* Small and stylish traditional-style guesthouse in a tranquil location near Westport's quays, half a mile from the town centre. There are four-poster beds and steam rooms available. Close to a good choice of pubs and restaurants.

Lakeland House € *Lisloughrey, Quay Road, Nr Cong, County Mayo, tel: (094) 954 6089, www.lakelandhouse.net.* Budget accommodation in a lovely spot, located near Lough Corrib and 1.5km (1 mile) from the pretty village of Cong, at the gateway to Connemara. Options include family rooms with en suite, through to shared dorms. Kitchen available for self-caterers.

WATERFORD

Granville Hotel €€ *Meagher Quay, Waterford, tel: (051) 305555,* www.gran
villehotel.ie. Situated along Waterford's quayside and with as many historical
connections as rooms, it's very popular with business travellers but makes a
great base for exploring the town.

Richmond House €€ *Cappoquin, County Waterford, tel: (058) 54278,* www.
richmondhouse.net. Beautiful country house with spacious rooms and period furnishings set in scenic grounds. Excellent restaurant serving Irish and
French cuisine.

Waterford Castle €€€ *The Island, Ballinakill, Waterford, tel: (051) 878203,*
www.waterfordcastleresort.com. Historic castle situated on its own private
island on the River Suir, surrounded by woodlands and an 18-hole championship golf course. Nineteen bright and airy bedrooms with stunning views
of the estate.

WEXFORD

Ferrycarrig Hotel €€€ *Wexford, tel: (053) 912 0999,* www.ferrycarrighotel.ie.
Each of the large, stylish rooms has a splendid view of the River Slaney estuary. Excellent riverside restaurant, bar, spa and leisure activities.

Kelly's Resort Hotel and Spa €€€ *Rosslare, County Wexford, tel: (053) 913
2114,* www.kellys.ie. Located on sandy Rosslare beach, this is one of Ireland's
great family-run hotels, with an excellent restaurant and spa.

NORTHWEST

Green Gate € *Ardvalley, Ardara, County Donegal, tel: (074) 954 1546,* www.
thegreengate.eu. This traditional cottage was bought by the proprietor as a
writer's retreat. Spend a night atop a hill on the edge of the Atlantic.

Markree Castle €€ *Collooney, Country Sligo tel: (071) 916 7800,* www.markree
castle.ie. Massive castellated mansion on a 400-hectare (1,000-acre) estate
of gardens and parkland that has been in the Cooper family for 350 years.

NORTHERN IRELAND

Belfast International Youth Hostel £ *22–32 Donegall Road, Belfast BT12 5JN, tel: (028) 9031 5435,* www.hini.org.uk. High-standard hostel in a central location (no need to have a membership card to stay).

Bushmills Inn £–££ *9 Dunluce Road, Bushmills, County Antrim BT 57 8QG, tel: (028) 2073 3000,* www.bushmillsinn.com. This place has all the ingredients of a great Irish holiday – whiskey, comfy beds, and great breakfasts – plus the Giant's Causeway is only 3km (2 miles) away.

Culloden Estate and Spa ££–£££ *142 Bangor Road, Holywood, County Down, tel: (028) 9042 1066,* www.hastingshotels.com/culloden-estate-and-spa. Northern Ireland's most luxurious hotel overlooks Belfast Lough. A glass cabinet lists famous names that have stayed here – they've all signed plastic yellow ducks (each room has one for the bath).

Europa ££–£££ *Great Victoria Street, Belfast BT2 7AP, tel: (028) 9027 1066,* www.hastingshotels.com/europa-belfast/. Next to the Grand Opera House, a 5-minute walk to the Golden Mile. Spacious elegance and stylish comfort, not to mention an interesting history (the 'most bombed hotel in the world', having suffered 36 bomb attacks during the Troubles, but has also hosted many famous gusts, including Bill Clinton).

Malmaison Belfast £££ *34-8 Victoria Street, tel: (028) 9600 1405,* www.malmaison.com. Warehouse conversion near the city centre and the Cathedral Quarter with bordello-themed rooms and an art deco-bar.

Ten Square Hotel ££ *10 Donegall Square South, tel: (028) 9024 1001,* www.tensquare.co.uk. A listed Victorian linen warehouse has been transformed into an ultra-luxury hotel with oriental decor and an emphasis on style. Right in the centre of town at Donegall Square.

La Mon Hotel and Country Club ££ *41 Gransha Road, Castlereagh, tel (028) 9044 8631,* www.lamon.co.uk. An oasis of calm that's ideal for families with tennis, swimming, putting green, kids club, and babysitting service. Spacious rooms with every modern comfort.

INDEX

THE **MINI** ROUGH GUIDE TO
IRELAND

First Edition 2022

Editor: Kate Drynan
Author: Ken Bernstein
Copyeditor: Philippa MacKenzie
Picture Editor: Tom Smyth
Cartography Update: Carte
Layout: Rebeka Davies
Head of DTP and Pre-Press: Katie Bennett
Head of Publishing: Kate Drynan
Photography Credits: Brian Morrison/Fáilte Ireland 45; Brian Morrison/NITB Photographic Library 5M; Catherine Mc Cluskey/Dublin Regional Tourism 37; Chris Hill/Tourism Ireland 7T, 57, 81, 82; Corrie Wingate/Apa Publications 28, 31, 32, 64, 66, 69, 77, 79, 91, 97, 103; Fáilte Ireland 5T, 4ML, 6T, 6B, 53; G Mitchel 86; Gareth Byrne Photography 26; Glyn Genin/Apa Publications 43, 47, 55, 59, 61, 63; Ireland Tourist Board 39, 40, 70, 72, 74, 88; iStock 24, 34; Kevin Cummins/Apa Publications 84, 92, 100, 106; Liam Murphy/Fáilte Ireland 49, 51; NITB Photographic Library 7B, 95, 105; Shutterstock 1, 4TL, 4ML, 5T, 5M, 5M, 5M, 5T, 11, 12, 15, 17, 18, 20
Cover Credits: Mizen Head **Monicami/Shutterstock**

Distribution
UK, Ireland and Europe: Apa Publications (UK) Ltd; sales@roughguides.com
United States and Canada: Ingram Publisher Services; ips@ingramcontent.com
Australia and New Zealand: Booktopia; retailer@booktopia.com.au
Worldwide: Apa Publications (UK) Ltd; sales@roughguides.com

Special Sales, Content Licensing and CoPublishing
Rough Guides can be purchased in bulk quantities at discounted prices. We can create special editions, personalised jackets and corporate imprints tailored to your needs. sales@roughguides.com; http://roughguides.com

Contact us
Every effort has been made to provide accurate information in this publication, but changes are inevitable. The publisher cannot be held responsible for any resulting loss, inconvenience or injury sustained by any traveller as a result of information or advice contained in the guide. We would appreciate it if readers would call our attention to any errors or outdated information, or if you feel we've left something out. Please send your comments with the subject line "Rough Guide Mini Ireland Update" to mail@uk.roughguides.com.